MW01045464

Next Stop! Tips & Tales From A Train Commuter

Next Stop! Tips & Tales From A Train Commuter

Thomas W. Macdonald

Copyright 2010 © Thomas W. Macdonald
ISBN 978-0-557-31438-6

Acknowledgements
&
Dedications

This book is dedicated to the many train commuters who get up early every morning and begin their day in darkness, braving the elements and making their journey to work, secure in a long, racing tube, only to do it in reverse at the end of a long day at work.

Special thanks go to my wife Corinne, my sons and my many friends and relatives who supported me, shared their experiences and proved invaluable in the editing and proofing of this book.

Finally, I want to give recognition to Aileen of 3amWriters, for helping bring color and visibility to my stories and more importantly, for her ongoing encouragement and enthusiasm that showed me how rewarding writing can be.

Table of Contents

Introduction ix

1. How I Got Here..1

2. What I Know About Trains 5

3. Unusual Happenings On The Platform...............9

4. Expect The Unexpected 13

5. Here's Looking At You.....................................21

6. Daily Doubler 25

7. Day Tripper 33

8. Stealth Rider 39

9. First, You Address The Ball............................43

10. Creatures Of Habit vs. Power Of Choice...........51

11. Fail To Plan, Plan To Fail.............................59

12. The Quest Begins 65

13. Ok, I'm On The Train, Now What? 71

14. You've made It! You Have Arrived!................77

15. Tourists Are People Too.................................81

16. Terminus 85

Introduction

A few years ago, I thought taking a train to work was an easy thing. After all, you just get on in one place and get off in another, right? Simple!

Several years of commuting by train from Milford, CT to New York City on the Metro North line have taught me just how wrong my initial impression was. This book is an attempt to help you, the reader, learn from my mistakes instead of making them yourself. (I'm sure you'd much rather make your own, unique mistakes. Or make none at all. Dare to dream!)

I am not an historian, a social scientist or even a railroad buff (more about those guys later.) I hope to help you see some humor in train travel, and pick up some tips that should help for a more enjoyable ride. This book may be helpful to anyone that may currently ride the trains regularly, or anyone who's just landed a fabulous new job that happens to be a train ride away from their home. Much of what is presented here can be used for any train line, not only Metro North. If nothing else, you can read this book on the train, and make your trip go by a little faster.

But if, like I was, you're facing the idea of taking the train on a daily basis and are new to the experience, my advice to you is do your homework, experiment, finalize your strategy and execute your plan.

Or, you can just get on and get off.

1. How I Got Here

If life is a journey (and every greeting card tells me it is), then my own working life can best be described through the different modes of transportation I've taken during my career. For me, it's been a journey of time, choice, and change. And all of it ended up with me, sitting in a big metal box hurtling to New York City alongside strangers on their own journeys, at the crack of a winter dawn a few years ago.

Yes, I'm a train commuter.

I didn't start out that way. After I graduated from college in 1977, I spent 15 years working for companies that sold mainframe computers to the business community. I was constantly on the road, visiting clients all over southern Connecticut and parts of Westchester County. Now, for a young person, especially a young guy, this was the ideal job.

When you're on the road for work, you are on your own a lot, only seeing your boss once in a while. Getting paid to enjoy this kind of freedom made me feel like a king, traveling in my mobile castle, a white Ford Mustang II T-Roof convertible. Strewn with sales materials and documents, a change of clothes and my golf clubs in the trunk, this car was all I needed. Thoughts seldom ranged beyond the present moment.

Back then there was no FM2, satellite, iPod, or MP3, but I did have one additional feature, my 8-track player. I could choose any station I wanted on my AM/FM radio. But when I could not find the music I wanted on the radio, I simply threw in one of my 8-track tapes and sang along.

Now for those of you who've never heard of an 8-track tape, it was the music world's first venture beyond reel-to-reel. This is not a history of the 8-track, though I'm sure that would be interesting and enlightening to us all, so I'll end by saying this: Yes, it was clunky. No, it did not rewind. This is why it was quickly replaced by tape cassettes, and then CD's, and the list goes on. But it did something important for us in the 70's that kids growing up today with iPods and music on their cell phones take for granted: *it gave us a choice.*

Back then, I spent my days driving, listening to my music, with the sun on my arms (in 1977, we did not yet realize that the sun was out to get us) and the wind in my face. I could go where I wanted, when I wanted. If I ate lunch and dinner on the road, or had to stay out late to meet with a client, or get an start early in the morning, it was no big deal. Time was not a concern, freedom was—and logging windshield miles provided that freedom. I averaged about 18,000 miles per year on my car, but who cared? Gas was cheap (compared to today anyways). It was my world and I loved it.

But as I grew older, time became more important. Freedom started to look different. Driving all over the map for hours every day lost its romance, became a barrier to the things I wanted to do. Part of this came about because of a major change that happened in my life: I started a family. Corinne and I were married in the spring of 1980, and anyone can tell you that was one of the happiest (and luckiest) days of my life. Soon after, we had our boys, Ryan and Justin.

With a suburban, ranch-style castle full of people I loved, I didn't feel the need to spend so much time in my kingdom on wheels. I realized the king could have a better time coaching baseball for the princes, or hanging out with the queen. Or perhaps, with a little more time in the day, the king could escape for a round of golf with fellow rulers from neighboring kingdoms. I decided to look for a job near home so that I could be where I wanted to be, when I wanted to be.

I was fortunate to land a job with one of my clients. Their office was less than 8 miles from my house and I could be at work within 15 minutes every morning. Even better, I could be home in the same amount of time, at a consistent hour every evening. There were other benefits of working so close to home, like the savings on maintenance and gasoline. So I settled into, and reveled in, my short commute. I had come 180 degrees. I no longer wanted the excessive travel time, and singing along with the music became secondary to reaching my destination. I even began listening to talk radio.

Without realizing it, I had become my parents. (It'll happen to you, too, if it hasn't already.)

Then, on October 2, 2006, I was informed that my services were no longer needed at the company I had called home for thirteen years.

Now, changing jobs in this era of dual-income households and corporate reorganization is not uncommon. Unlike years ago where the father/husband was the primary breadwinner and likely worked one job his entire life, in today's society, changing jobs is accepted, if not expected. But doing so involuntarily introduces a whole new dynamic. *It removes the choice.*

As I progressed through my career, I considered looking for new work from time to time, even though I usually ended up feeling satisfied to stay where I was. When you already have a job, you can be selective. You can look for all the things that are important to you: money, challenge, benefits, future opportunity, and location. But when you are suddenly unemployed and are forced to find a job, you no longer feel that control over your choices. When the main priority is "find work," you quickly find out how flexible you can really be. And no one realized this more than I did.

After 4 months of unemployment, I found a great job with an internationally known consulting firm. The good news: I was working again. The bad news: I was now working in lower Manhattan. My 15 minute commute in the comfort and privacy of my car had become a journey spanning two and a half hours and involving four modes of transportation: car, train, subway and foot. The trip now became a major part of my day. No more getting in my car, turning on the radio and hitting the road. I now had to get to the train station, park my car, buy my ticket, find a seat, and ride for 90 minutes. And this was just to get to Grand Central Station. Once there, I still had a subway ride facing me, followed by a walk to my office, at that time in winter weather. The comfort of the train ride quickly became integral to the overall satisfaction of my day.

When I began my new job in New York and was faced with taking the train into the city, I did not think I had any cause for worry or anxiety. After all, I was a grown man who had made this trip on several occasions while working in my previous job. I knew where to get on the train and where to get off, I mean, really, that's all that matters, right? Well, that may be true for most, but as I quickly found out, it was not true for me.

See, taking the train once in a while is not the same as taking it every day. It requires an entirely different mindset, and a level of patience and tolerance that I soon realized did not reside in me. By the end of the first week, after five straight days commuting by train into the city, I had had enough! I got off the train that Friday night and swore I would never, EVER take the train again.

I told my wife that evening that I was quitting, that NO job was worth that commute. But after dinner and some calming rationale from Corinne (prompted, I'm sure, by her more realistic appraisal of what our finances would look like once my severance pay ended, and supplemented by her generously-poured glasses of wine) I calmed down enough to rethink my position. After all, millions of people take the train on a daily basis, and live to tell the tale. I knew I would have to adjust, refine my approach to make the commute more tolerable, maybe even enjoyable. At that point, I was grasping at straws—making a train ride enjoyable seemed like a goal hitherto only achieved in children's stories and nursery rhymes.

I attacked the problem with renewed energy that weekend, and began my one-man study of how to deal with a train commute. I researched, I experimented, I observed. I found that even though it felt like my choices had been narrowed, I did have a choice as to how I dealt with my daily commute. I wasn't the young guy with the wind in his hair anymore, or the contented guy with the 15-minute commute, but I could still find a way enjoy the journey.

This is what has led me to writing this book. I wanted to share my observations and experiences while riding the train every day for two years, and humbly offer a few tips to my fellow commuters. Not every tip will be for everyone. You may even come up with some of your own. If you're an experienced commuter, you probably already have many tips of your own, and you may recall funny incidents you experienced yourself but had forgotten over the years. Or you may catch yourself thinking *hey, I never realized that but he's right!* As you will see in the next chapter, being right is an experience I normally reserve for my wife, but I enjoy it once in a while, too.

2. What I Know About Trains

From the time trains first began running in the United States, the railroads have been a key thread of the American fabric. Railroads have moved people, goods, and livestock for hundreds of years and millions of miles. They have provided employment for many and enjoyment for even more. They have shaped American history in many ways. However, they didn't really catch my interest until I was forced to sit in one for upwards of three hours a day.

As a kid growing up in the small town of Thomaston, Connecticut, the original home of Seth Thomas Clocks, my time was consumed with sports. Some little boys love trains and cars and things on wheels but I was not one of them. Transportation was nothing other than a way to get somewhere. I had no interest in trains, planes, or even boats. It was not until later in life that I learned about railroads, and my education was largely at the hands of people who knew and loved trains.

One of my first experiences with railroads occurred while my wife, Corinne, and I were newlyweds. She was from a small town in southwestern Pennsylvania, and every few weeks we would travel there to spend the weekend with her family. We traveled by car, leaving Connecticut late Friday afternoon and driving through New York, New Jersey, and most of Pennsylvania. The trip was supposed to last about six-and-a-half hours, but with Friday night traffic through the metropolitan area and the seemingly never-ending road construction through Pennsylvania, the trip often took up to eight hours.

At the end of our trip, with just a mile or two to go, we would enter into her hometown of Hyndman, Pennsylvania and have to cross a set of railroad tracks in the middle of town. Usually this signaled the home stretch, and I was jubilant at the prospect of getting out of the car, stretching my legs, and attending to those bodily functions that are often postponed during a long car trip through towns where the only choice of rest stop is a small, dark, gas station bathroom. On this one night, however, as we approached the tracks with the end of our journey in sight, with bells ringing and lights flashing, the long white and black striped crossing guards slowly descended in front of us. A train was approaching.

Now, having been brought up in the sophisticated suburbs of Connecticut, I saw an opportunity to show my new bride from the hills of Pennsylvania just how cultured and worldly I was. I looked to my right and said, "I bet I can guess how many cars are on this train." She took my challenge with a smile that I would later come to know as her "My husband is a sweet man, so I tolerate his moments of stupidity" smile. I thought back to the largest train I could remember seeing back home, and estimated in my mind there were about 10 cars on that train.

Remember, as a young boy, I didn't have much exposure to trains. I wasn't into trains like some boys are, I was into sports. There was a train track that ran along the river in Thomaston but I don't recall ever seeing a train on it. Whenever I did see a train, it was a passenger train—with maybe 10 cars full of people, moving smoothly along, clickety-clack. Here, in the upper Appalachian Mountains, in the middle of the night, it was clear this was no passenger train: this was a freight train pulling coal cars; big, heavy, dirty coal cars. I reasoned that there must be more cars on a freight train than a typical passenger train. I took a wild risk and doubled the number. I was full of confidence as I looked her in the eye and guessed, "20 cars."

The count began. 1, 2, 3.... 10, 11, 12... My enthusiasm grew as I approached the magic number and my chance to establish the male as the gender of superior intelligence at a critical point in my young marriage. Watching with great excitement to my left as the cars passed by, I counted 18, 19, 20, 21, 22... NO CABOOSE! The cars kept coming and I kept counting. Finally, after car number 100 passed by, with the yawns coming more frequently and my bladder reaching the point of explosion, I sheepishly looked at Corinne. Being the kind and indulgent wife she was (and still is), she mastered her impulse to burst out laughing. She just sat there and smiled.

I never did figure out exactly how many cars were on that train. It wasn't the longest train in the world, but it sure as heck felt like it! (Note: the longest train on record ran on June 21, 2001 from Port Hedlund, Australia. This train had a total of 682 cars, pulled by 8 engines, and extended over 4.5 miles long.[1]) Luckily, for the next thirty

---

[1] http://thelongestlistofthelongeststuffatthelongestdomainnameatlonglast.com/long8.html

years, we never had to wait again, but better safe than sorry: I always make a pit stop before we get to those darn tracks.

I should not have been surprised that my wife knew how wrong my guess would prove to be. She had good reason to know about trains. At the turn of the century, Corinne's great-grandfather worked as an engineer on the railroads. His son (her grandfather, Guy Cook, Sr.) followed in his footsteps, working as the Station Manager in Garret, Pennsylvania. Corinne and her sister Vicki have cherished memories of spending time with their grandfather at the station back in the 1950's and 60's, trying out his state-of-the-art black typewriter and weighing themselves on the heavy-duty scales used to weigh shipments. Remember, no video games back then.

During the potato harvest each year, trains would haul the potatoes from the fields to the nearby Snyders of Berlin Potato Chip factory, and the station became a hive of activity, with Guy, Sr. handling it all. But the most important function he performed was the daily mail run. He would load up his hand-pump rail car with mailbags and manually pump the car along the track (careers like this are the reason that Americans didn't need workout videos and gym memberships until the last couple of decades). At the end of his journey, he would hang the mailbags on a hook. The train would pass by, slowing but never stopping. A person on the train would retrieve the outgoing mail as the train went by (and by "retrieve," I mean, "seize the mail off the hook and hope he didn't get yanked off the moving train") and toss the bag of incoming mail to the ground where her grandfather would pick it up and take it to the Post Office. At that time, this was a major component of the successful functioning of our postal system.

"Paple Cook" (as he was known to his grandchildren) often brought his own children to the station with him when they were young. They all pitched in, helping him with his daily duties. His son, Guy, Jr., developed a real fondness for these powerful vehicles. His home was decorated with train memorabilia and going to train shows was one of his favorite pastimes. I recall a trip the family took into Washington, DC on the metro rail service. He was about 75 years old, but his eyes shone with the excitement of a young child on his first ride.

The passion of railroad buffs and memorabilia collectors is second to none, so I would be remiss in writing any book about trains if I didn't tell you a bit about my old boss, Tim. This man knew more about trains than anyone I have ever known. Many times, he tried to share his wealth of information with me. And every time I listened with the enthusiasm we reserve for stories about things we are not personally interested in but are interesting to people who are important to us, i.e., people who would be signing our paychecks and deciding whether we received a promotion or not.

When I told Tim my wife grew up in a small town in southwestern Pennsylvania, located near Cumberland, Maryland, he went on to tell me more than I ever cared to know about Cumberland and its history. Evidently, Cumberland was a major train hub and served a critical role to the U.S. rail system, and therefore held Tim's interest to a large degree. It was from Tim that I learned obscure details such as the physics that govern braking on a downhill run, or the need to accelerate in advance to generate enough power in order to make it up a severe incline. Believe me, it's not like driving a car. Although it didn't make me a railroad buff —sorry, no converts here — it did help me begin to understand the complexity that goes on behind trains and railroads.

There are plenty of railroad books out there, and plenty of railroad enthusiasts who have read 'em all. Should you ever want to learn more about the railroad system and its history in our country, talk to someone who has this same fervor, who grew up with the railroads. But make sure you've got some time on your hands — they will give you a textbook's worth of information and a liberal dose of enthusiasm to boot!

3. Unusual Happenings On The Platform

Those of you who have not ridden the trains may think that there is nothing special about the platform. It's just another place to stand and wait. And for 99% of the time, that is true. But every once in a while, it can be the scene of some interesting episodes and events.

One cold winter morning, I was taking the 6:33 A.M. train. It was in the middle of winter, still dark and snowing. The crowd on the platform was awaiting the arrival of the southbound train to New York. We looked more like an Eskimo colony gathering for an ice-fishing expedition than a group of suburban commuters, waiting to take the train to our respective offices in the concrete wilderness.

That particular morning, people were bundled up to their eyes in overcoats, scarves, gloves, boots—if my own mother had been standing next to me in this garb, at that moment, I would not have recognized her. But it wasn't about looks, it was about survival. We were braving the elements for this experience, and we did anything we could do to keep ourselves from freezing until we could get inside the relative warmth and comfort of the train.

I looked around, taking in the station area as I waited, trying to get my mind off the cold. Across the tracks, on the northbound side, there were two men standing on the platform. Typically there is little traffic heading in the opposite direction, away from New York City, in the morning, so I was surprised to see anyone at all. I reasoned they must be traveling together, but they didn't have much luggage. It appeared that one of the men was holding something rather bulky, but not a briefcase or backpack. The other seemed to be holding something small in one hand.

A moment later, it became clear to me when the man holding the small object raised it to his face, while at the same time, the other lifted his bulky package up to his shoulder. It was then that I realized who they were. It was the local television weatherman out of New Haven, Connecticut, and his cameraman. They were broadcasting the weather from our train station.

Now I found this rather strange, because at my station in Milford, the weather isn't all that different from the one right near the news office in New Haven. I mean, we're talking a very small distance here, it's not like there was a blizzard in my town while the New Haven people were out having picnics and sunning themselves in the town square. I thought to myself, *you two could have made this report at the New Haven station, why on earth did you come here?*

Then, the thought occurred to me: oh, it's not just weather, it's a human interest story. They're trying to report the weather and show how it affects the local commuters, those who travel this way every day, in sun, rain, and snow. I felt proud to be a commuter at that moment, and I felt a sense of camaraderie. We weren't just poor unlucky slobs who had to take public transportation to work every day. We were pioneers blazing a trail through hardship, huddled together in our own modern-day version of a wagon train. It's not for everyone, I thought, but we are the tough ones, we can do it. I looked around at my fellow commuters, warmed by a glow of pride. I waited, too, for the reporters to cross to our platform and talk to us. Surely, they would want to get a firsthand account of what this is like, get our reactions to the weather, and hear our stories. Maybe I'd be on TV, and I could tell Corinne to tune in when she got home from work! I'd call my kids too, to see if they could tape the broadcast. Good ol' Dad on the news. Yeah!

I was so lost in my reverie that I was shocked into reality when the reporters suddenly gathered their gear and departed. I boarded the train without a chance to share my hard-won experiences of commuting in the sleet and snow. And I kept thinking about it as my train pulled out of the station, bound for New York—why on earth did they do that? If you were going to leave New Haven and travel to a remote station to broadcast from the train platform at 6:30 in the morning, in a blizzard and freezing cold, wouldn't you want to take time and maybe interview a few of the commuters? Isn't the point to see how it affects those people who brave these elements every day? And if that was your purpose, why did you set up on the NORTHBOUND side? Didn't you see there was NO ONE THERE?

I was also surprised how politics became integrated into the train commuters' lives. We have all seen how our local politicians turn out as Election Day approaches. We expect to see them argue in debates and schmooze in interviews, on television, in the newspapers, and even on the Internet. Political campaigns have been with us since the start of our nation. In many ways, it's what separates us from other countries around the world and what makes our nation so wonderful.

As our politicians try to influence your vote in their favor, you will see them show up at civic functions such as parades and festivals. It makes sense. These venues provide a forum for politicians to reach out to many diverse constituents. They will hand out flyers, shake your hand, kiss your baby. All tactics designed to get your vote. We see it, we understand it, we expect it.

Being new to the daily commuting routine, what I did not expect was the sudden appearance of politicians on the train platform, a day or two before Election Day. Apparently train commuters form a very large voting bloc that was kept secret until the last minute. As I observed how they befriended passengers preparing to board their train, it struck me how unique this group of voters was. Unlike those that turn out for civic functions, the people waiting on the platform share a common bond that has nothing to do with shared beliefs or political philosophy; we are commuters. We depend on the public transportation system every day to get us to work and back. I thought to myself, if only we could harness our powers for political pull, imagine what we might accomplish! Leather upholstery on the seats, iPod hookups at every window, free lattes distributed by the conductors...the possibilities are endless! Maybe we should create our own political party, The Commuter Party: Dedicated to Comfortable Conditions for Poor Unlucky People Who Take the Train to Work.

I do have to give politicians credit, though, they know their business and they know how to get the votes. What does almost every early morning commuter hanker for, as he or she stands and wait for the train? Coffee and donuts, right? Well, these politicians were no fools, they had a quantity of coffee and donuts the likes of which I have never seen, and they were handing them out like they were about to be declared illegal. Watching the candidates shaking hands, smiling, and distributing these valuable freebies, I imagined some memo probably got circulated years ago: For the effective promotion of candidates to the local commuter population, always utilize free coffee and donuts.

Traditionally I based my vote on a politician's positions and beliefs — what a fool I was! Rather than spend time reading up on the candidate's views and following campaign coverage, I could now simply base my vote on who had the best donut. Of course, politics is a fickle mistress. You can only imagine my disappointment when, on the day after the election, none of the winners showed up to say thank you and hand out any léftover donuts. I guess they had just the right amount to get the vote. My question is this: *is it scarier that a person may make their choice based on a free donut and cup of coffee, or, is it scarier that politicians actually think someone will?*

Oh well, so goes the political process in this grand country of ours. Note to any politicians that may be reading this book, I am easily swayed by a jelly donut, preferably strawberry.

4. Expect The Unexpected

Unfortunately, there are many things in life we cannot control. As much as we may wish we could, it is just not possible. For instance, we can't control when the sun rises and sets. Mother Nature takes care of that one. And we all know it's not nice to try to fool Mother Nature. Another example is the number of hours in the day (24, right?). But wait, let's think about that one. Why can't we change that? I mean, Mother Nature did not come up with that number. It wasn't handed down on tablets from on high, either. Who decided on a 24-hour day? I think it was some guy named Hipparchus.[2] What did he know about trying to balance work and family and maintain a career in an ever-shifting modern capitalist economy? He was from ancient Greece, for crying out loud!

Granted, 24 hours does work out well for everyone, we're used to it by now. It lets us know when to eat breakfast, lunch and dinner, when to watch our favorite show, when to go to bed and get up in the morning. Hey, what did people do before Hipparchus came along? How did they know when to eat? How would they know when to go to bed? Hipparchus must have had a lot of free time on his hands to figure this one out. But how much free time did he have if he had not invented hours yet? Oh well, I guess it's too late to change now. But we all have had days that we wish would never end and those that could not end soon enough.

Anyway, let's get back on track (excuse the train pun), where were we? Oh, yeah, things we can't control. There are many things we cannot control, and many of them can have an impact on train travel and our ability to follow some of the suggestions that will be discussed in later chapters. Fog, snow, and ice have all been known to wreak havoc on train schedules. Ice on the tracks and overhead wires (because some trains run by electric power) can cause outages and delays. Trains may

---

[2] http://curious.astro.cornell.edu/question.php?number=594

be forced to take alternative measures as they strive to maintain the best service possible during terrible conditions. Express routes may become local, additional cars may be added if possible. In some severe cases where trains cannot get through, buses may be provided as an alternate means of transportation. They may have to cancel some trains, and of course, fewer trains running leads to more people crowding onto the existing ones.

The point is, that even though you may think that you'll get on the train at Point A and ride smoothly along until you exit the train at Point B, that may not always occur. In such situations, it is quite possible that you will not reach your destination on time, and that along the way, you will undergo some mild-to-moderate insults to your sense of comfort. Guess what? You cannot control the situation!

Another thing that you cannot control is your destination. Now, you may not agree with this. After all, you are the one choosing to take the train and determining where you are headed. You see the direction and get on the train, thinking you are all set. You can argue all you want with me on this one, but what you must understand is that trains don't stop in every town. You might think that the train is going to stop in your town. You know it has to go through your town to reach the destination on the board, so why wouldn't it just stop and let you out? But, the train is not as flexible as one might like it to be. The train is going to stop at all the prescribed stops on its route and that's it. It's not like the bus, where you can pull a string and get off a few blocks before your street. So you have to make absolutely sure that the train you're getting on is stopping at the station you want, or you will have the highly frustrating experience of watching your station whiz by before your eyes. While you may want to take an express train in order to save time, you may be forced to take a local train that stops in the town, or closest to the town you are trying to reach.

Then, of course, there is the occurrence of every lawyer's favorite, **Force Majeure**. This phrase, seen most often in legal documents, refers to natural disasters or other "Acts of God". Simply put, it is a fancy, official-sounding way of describing events that are not only out of your control, but vastly inconvenient and possibly dangerous.

I experienced (and was duly inconvenienced by) a **Force Majeure** on March 4, 2008. On this day, I happened to arrive at Grand Central Station at approximately 3:30 P.M., hoping to catch the next express and get home a little early. I had that spring in my step as I got off the subway, anticipating walking in the door, being able to have a nice, leisurely dinner with Corinne, share a bottle of wine, maybe even take a walk around the neighborhood—after all, it would still be *light* out when I got home! That was my plan. All I needed was to get on the next express train to New Haven.

When I got off the subway and walked upstairs into the main lobby at Grand Central, I froze in my jaunty tracks. Something was off. The place was full with people, as usual. But instead of the normal scene of people rushing to trains and running to ticket booths, there was stillness. There was no hustle and bustle, nothing, just people, lots of them, standing still, many with a look of puzzlement on their faces.

I looked at the big board on the wall over the ticket booths and saw that the train schedule was strangely...blank. Not sure what to do, I did what any person with an ounce of common sense does when they want information: I headed for the information booth. Before I reached the information booth, however, an official announcement boomed out over the motionless, murmuring crowd:

"Attention please: All rail service has been suspended indefinitely. Repeat: All rail service has been suspended indefinitely. Thank you."

Well, that pretty much scrapped my plan. And what's more, I (along with all the other train riders) had no idea what to do next. We didn't know what happened at first, and once we got a tidbit of information, we played a business-person version of that childhood favorite, the telephone game. You know, the one that occurs whenever you're in a crowd and nobody knows what's going on, and everyone is starting to get impatient and nervous. Word quickly spread that a building had collapsed at 124th street. Lacking any accurate information, the rumors started to take on a life of their own.

Did you hear that a building exploded? The tracks are covered with debris. It will take weeks to uncover them. They have to send a special work crew in. Was anyone hurt? We have no idea. Oh, dear. I heard the tracks are damaged beyond repair. They may have to close the station at 125th street entirely. Oh, that's terrible! Did you hear that there may have been toxic waste expelled into the atmosphere? Yeah, it ate through the tracks. Vats of fluorescent green nuclear stuff, like in that movie, what was it called? We could all be in danger. It's a conspiracy, you know. The airlines and the auto industry are getting together to bring down the rail service. They're threatened by us. It's all a conspiracy.

Fortunately, none of these rumors were true, and most importantly, no. one was injured. It seems that the building was unoccupied and had deteriorated to the point that it collapsed under its own weight. Rail service was suspended until officials were convinced that there was no damage to the rails and that stability of the rails was not compromised.

All told, service was suspended from approximately 3:15PM until 4:45PM. It was only an hour and a half, but it was during peak service hours, so Metro North officials had to work doubly hard to get the trains running as quickly as possible.

So, due to this *Force Majeure*, my plan of getting home a little early did not pan out quite as I had hoped. So I went to Plan B. I called Corinne, told her what I knew and that I may end up staying in the city for the night. I thought about going to one of the many eateries in Grand Central and partaking of train station cuisine (which, to my pleasant surprise, is not that bad, there are several selections ranging from hot dogs to full menus of national and international cuisine, the quality of which ranges from decently edible to surprisingly tasty).

My Plan B was called into question when rumor spread that service might be back soon. I then developed another plan, which could be seen as a version of my earlier Plan A, but will for purposes of clarity now be known as Plan C: I decided to wait it out, and shortly after, I was rewarded with this announcement:

"Attention please: Conditions have been resolved. Train service will soon resume as scheduled. Repeat: Conditions have been resolved, and your regular train service will soon resume. Thank you."

Hearing that service was to be restored, I moved from Plan C to Plan D. The objective of Plan D was to be on the first train home, and the execution of this plan required me to be in a location from which I could not only hear announcements, but be able follow the announcement's directives easily. I decided to forego my desire for sustenance and position myself for a seat on the first train heading to New Haven. I knew the terrain. I knew the conditions. The first train would be very crowded, so I would have to act quickly but carefully. I assumed an air of casual purpose as I meandered to the North side of the upper level, where the train platforms are located. No rush, just quickly and quietly moving to the high ground. I was ready. As soon as the departing train's track number was announced, I would be able to make my move. Because I'd chosen this advantageous spot, I would be one of the first on board. I was determined. Plan D was going to work.

When the first train to depart was announced, I was ready to pounce. However, to my disappointment, the first train was headed for points north of the city, <u>not</u> the New Haven line. (Remember what I said about the ability to choose your destination?) I don't think I even knew there was a line that goes north. You can imagine the letdown. But I shook off my disappointment and got ready for the next announcement.

With the first announcement, there came a mass movement of people towards the north side. As the crowd grew, my personal space, there on the spot of advantage, shrunk. Then, word spread that the first New Haven-bound train would be departing from the lower level.

As soon as I heard this, I put Plan E (get to the train in its new location as quickly as possible) into action, turned and headed for the stairs. Since I was located close to the stairwell (thanks to the successful implementation of Plan D), I was one of the first to reach the lower level and secure a spot near the gate. Ha! I beat them all again. I held my ground in the growing crowd of people that had surged down the stairs in response to the same rumor. Now I knew Plan E was the one: once the New Haven train was announced, I would be one of the first to enter the track area, find MY seat and settle in. We waited with bated breath for another announcement, but it was the Harlem line, AGAIN!

Still the crowd stayed calm, although I was now getting a little more frustrated. After what seemed an eternity, they made the announcement for the New Haven Line:

"*Attention please......*".

My frustration was about to end.

"*The train to New Haven.....*"

C'mon, c'mon, what track number?

"*making all local stops......*"

I don't care if it stops every mile, just tell me what track!

"*will depart from track........*"

You're killing me...........WHAT TRACK?

"*25, on the upper level*"

The upper level, UPPER LEVEL? You've got to be kidding me. *"Thank you."*
Well, you are NOT welcome!

Plan E was soon replaced with a furious scramble to avoid getting crushed in the crowd now headed to the New Haven train. All the planning, anticipation, positioning had been a waste of time. Standing in the front of the crowd at the lower level tracks, I turned to head up the stairs only to see a mass of human beings doing the same. Except, they were all in FRONT of me this time. Not bothering to figure out what plan I was now on, I was down to my last option: make my way up the stairs to track 25 and begin walking the platform, peering in the windows of each car in search of a seat, any seat. My hopes faded as I passed car after car, unable to locate a spot for me. It appeared increasingly that I was destined to stand for the 90 minute ride home. But I moved onward, continuing my search. And as I did so, it struck me how much longer this train was. What I realized was that the highly trained operation people at Metro North were prepared for such a disaster. They had a plan of their own. They had expected the unexpected and when hit with it, reacted quickly to add extra cars to accommodate the unending flow of tired, hungry commuters. Despite the many alternative plans that I came up with, it was their plan that saved my fate. Add more cars. How ingenious! I soon came upon a car that still had several unoccupied seats and entered it immediately. I jumped into the first row I saw and planted myself in the empty seat by the window for the long ride home. Schedules no longer mattered, heck they no longer existed. As soon as all the riders were boarded, the train left the station. The majority of riders found seats, but many were forced to stand.

What I had hoped to be a short day, surprising my wife with an early homecoming, ended up being one of the longest days of my commuting history.

This type of event is very rare, at least in my two years of rail experience. But it taught me a lot about being willing to change, and to go with the flow. And what it taught me is something I never would have learned without undergoing my commuting experience. I realized, that no matter what conditions exist, I still would recommend taking the train whenever possible. And this event is evidence of the reason why. The dedication and commitment of train personnel to provide quality service no matter what the circumstances.

Thinking back to this day, I remember how people behaved. Human beings don't always accept change easily, and an unplanned event such as this one can bring out the worst in us. The majority of travelers at that time of day are leaving the city, heading home at the end of a busy day at work. They're tired and hungry. Understandably, people are eager to board their train and get home. I know I was.

A lengthy delay such as this may cause some dismay, frustration, even annoyance. As I observed the crowd around me, I saw all of these, but what was noticeably absent was anger. I saw none of that. And an event such as this, where there seems to be little explanation and information supplied, can be frightening for people. It was confusing, and some people were not sure what to do. But there was no panic or disruption.

As more people entered Grand Central, unaware of the delays and hoping to catch their train, the lobby area became increasingly crowded. More people had to hear the story and go to their own personal Plan B, again and again. Still, everyone remained calm. It gave me a sense of reassurance about people in general, that we can adjust when it's necessary, and we don't have to throw tantrums when our plans go off track. This is the kind of lesson we only learn when we're in a big crowd of people with the same goal in mind, up against the same challenges.

And that's the lesson I learned from train travel that day. Expect the unexpected, and be prepared to change your plan, smile, and move on. You can come up with Plan A, B, or even Plan Z, but the reality is, whatever your plan, if you just stay cool and do what the booming voice says, you'll eventually get to your destination.

5. Here's Looking At You

One of the most famous lines ever spoken in a movie was by Humphrey Bogart, in the movie *Casablanca*, when he bade goodbye to Ingrid Bergman with the words, "Here's looking at you, kid." At the risk of showing my age, that is my all-time favorite movie, so I decided to use that line for this chapter title. Call it author's prerogative. Hopefully you will understand why as you read on. If not, you are probably only reading this book because your dad or your uncle who commute by train to work gave it to you as a graduation gift as a hint to go get yourself a job, pronto. And if that's you, you should see *Casablanca* anyway, it's a classic!

How many of you like people-watching? Seriously, admit it, you do, don't you? We all do. It's one of humanity's favorite pastimes, me included. As a hobby, it offers the ultimate in ease and convenience. You don't need any equipment except your own eyes and your imagination. It can be done almost anywhere, and when teamed up with waiting, it is a great way to pass the time. That's probably why I employed my keen interest and skill in people-watching when I began to commute by train, because commuting by train involves a great deal of waiting. You wait at the ticket booth, you wait to get on the train, you wait to get a seat, you wait to get off the train, you wait, wait, wait....

Anyway, about people-watching.

My guess is that people-watching has been going on since the beginning of time, starting with Adam and Eve. Since they only had each other to look at, it was probably called person-watching, or just plain staring. I wonder how many times one of them said, "Hey, what are you staring at?" Being the only two people alive, it probably became pretty boring over time. Maybe not in the beginning, but when they started wearing those fig leaves, the hobby likely lost its appeal. On the other hand, the addition of these rudimentary clothes may have actually increased the excitement, as now the imagination added some spice to the process.

By the way, we only ever hear of Adam and Eve wearing fig leaves. Why is that? We know there were other trees. I mean, there was an *apple* tree, right? (At least according to popular imaginings of the fateful fruit.) Okay, so maybe wearing a leaf from that tree would have been inappropriate. What about other trees? Did they ever consider wearing a maple tree leaf? Maybe it would have more coverage, or add a Canadian flair to their attire. But seeing as this was before Canada and before everything else altogether, maybe the maple leaf was only brought out on formal occasions.

Then, of course, think of the Roman Empire. As one of the world's first melting pots, made up of numerous diverse ethnic, social, and religious groups, Rome probably offered an abundant opportunity for observing others. When people gathered in the Coliseum for an afternoon of gladiator battles and the feeding of Christians to the lions, seating was assigned by social class, with the poor located in the higher sections. The lower sections with the better view were reserved for the wealthy. (Kind of like a professional baseball game today.) In ancient Rome, clothes, along with seating location, revealed the status of the individual.

You could imagine the spectators in the higher sections looking down at the wealthy and commenting on their wardrobe:

"Look at those snobs in their fancy togas, while I am sitting here in my rags."

"I wonder where they shop."

"She looks awful in that color, and those sandals, yuck."

"Who wears a Stola to a chariot race?"

In today's world, a prime place for people-watching is the shopping mall, especially for men. This is because everyone knows that men and women have entirely different agendas and methods when it comes to shopping. It can be summed up in one word: browsing. Women do it. Men do not. Next time you are in a mall, look around and see how many men are waiting outside a store while their wives or girlfriends are inside shopping (read: *browsing*.) What are these men doing to relax and pass the time? It's not like they brought a book with them or anything! They're people-watching. My father-in-law and I have made people-watching a team sport, because of the many times we've had to we take our wives to the mall near Corinne's home town. On one occasion, he pointed out to me a gentleman that happened to be the brother of a very popular and talented pitching coach for a major league baseball team. That was a very successful bout of people-watching, definitely a candidate for the People-watching Hall of Fame.

So, being a man who has accompanied my own better half on countless shopping excursions, I was already practiced at people-watching. But my train commuting experience made me a positive prodigy at it. People-watching can be as interesting as you want it to be. You can make a game out of it, or several games, depending on how long you are waiting around. My personal go-to game was always Guess-the-Job.

You would think this game would be easy on a train full of commuters, but let me tell you, it takes intense powers of observation and skill. Sure, everyone is commuting to his or her own place of work, but what does that mean? Where are they going, what building, what career? Is the guy wearing overalls and carrying a helmet working on a bridge or maybe the 50th floor of a new high-rise building under construction? Why is the other man in a suit today when he normally is dressed business casual? Is the man in the plain gray suit a lawyer, a finance genius headed for Wall Street? Wait, fancy tie...he could be in advertising. What about the woman next to him, dressed in a black suit, nylons, and the requisite sneakers? Are they coworkers? Complete strangers? Coworkers having a secret affair at risk to their jobs, so they are forced to pretend to be complete strangers outside of work, lest they be spied fraternizing on the morning commute? You may never know the answer but just letting your mind wander can be fun. Everyone has a story, and the beauty of people-watching is that *you* can make it up *for* them!

People-watching on the train is entertaining, but it does require a certain technique beyond the typical mall-variety people-watching. The diversity of riders makes for many a story, but the layout of the terrain poses challenges at times. People waiting for the train are lined up along the platform and usually facing forward. To truly observe, you must look to your left and right, and you must do so without being too obvious. I honed my observational skills, trying to make sidelong glances long enough to gather information to feed my curiosity, but not long enough to attract the attention of the observed subject. You see, while we all like to people-watch, we never want to get caught doing it, right?

It's interesting what you see while waiting for the train. During weekdays, most riders are commuters. They tend to stand in the same place every day. Some will read the paper while waiting. There is very little conversation. - On the other hand, tourists tend to travel in groups and so there is more chatter among them. They also can be often seen fumbling with the ticket machine as they attempt to purchase their tickets in advance. But in all cases, people tend to be patient and courteous, and that's a good thing.

Weekend travel is primarily made up of tourists. They may be young couples off on a day of romance, families with excited young children, or older, more mature people. Trying to guess where they are headed or what their plans are can be another game. Are they going to a show, a ball game, shopping, sightseeing? Sometimes it's easy. They provide more clues, maybe a camera, or wearing a favorite team baseball jersey or carrying a brochure or two. Other times it is not. But it sure passes the time.

Watching parents deal with young children always brought mixed feelings for me. I'd see them on the platform, the parents as eager and wound up as the children, everyone ready for an adventure. I felt happy for them as I remembered many such excursions with my own children. I also shook my head and thought, *You poor fools. Look at you, trying to explain to your 5-year-old son why he can't lie down and peek over the gold line to see the tracks. And now the 8-year-old is teasing the 3-year old. Did you really think you had a hope of containing these frenzied, fearless whirls of activity?* Ah, memories!

Over time, as I refined my people-watching style, I began to take note of the diversity of train riders, and created a kind of shorthand code to describe each type of rider I saw frequently.

The train riding population is composed of workers, students, and tourists. There are professionals and laborers; elderly and infants. People bring briefcases, bags, laptops, bicycles, even strollers. Some prefer a window seat, others the aisle. Some even prefer to stand, although I have *no* idea why. Maybe it's some religious devotion or self-flagellation, to stand for an hour when there is an empty seat right at your knee. Some like to talk, others read, listen to music, or sleep (my favorite).

After studying the different types of riders, I have broken them down into three categories. The next three chapters discuss each of these groups, how they differ, and the characteristics that are common for each group. Happy people-watching!

6. Daily Doubler

The first category is made up of people that ride the train every day, twice a day, hence the name Daily Doubler. This passenger likely makes up the majority of the train riders during the peak hours of the normal workday. In other words, this person is the daily commuter. They see the ride as simply a means of transportation, a necessary and neutral part of their normal workday routine. The novelty of the train ride for them has worn off long ago.

In many ways, the train ride is like riding in an elevator, except it goes horizontally. Notice this the next time you get in an elevator: few people make conversation with fellow riders. You'll only be there a short while, it's a means to an end. Why strike up a conversation that will only be interrupted by arriving at your floor minutes later? There's really only time for a quick smile and nod, and if you're tired, focused on getting to your office so you can begin work, and it's a gray, rainy Monday morning...well, you can imagine that most of the Daily Doublers riding in this giant, public version of the elevator aren't much for conversation. They tend to keep to themselves, don't talk much unless riding with an associate or a friend. When they do talk, they speak quietly, making an effort to keep their conversations private and not disturb others.

The Daily Doubler tends to follow train etiquette more faithfully than the other groups. They are well prepared for the ride, having developed a routine they follow with a strictness bordering on the obsessive-compulsive.

Here is a list of the characteristics associated with your typical Daily Doubler that I like to call my "3 A's": Attire, Accoutrements, Attitude.

Attire

Daily Doublers generally wear suits or "business casual" clothing and business shoes. They also don weather-appropriate outerwear, e.g., umbrellas, raincoats, overcoats, hats, gloves, scarves. Many of them are stylish but mostly, it's about protecting yourself from the elements, and they have long abandoned any qualms about looking strange if they have to bundle up to wait on a snowy train platform.

The Daily Doubler of the non-corporate variety is easily recognizable by their wardrobe of denim pants, tee shirts, sweatshirts, work boots, and a construction helmet if their job requires one. You won't often see this rider with an umbrella (at least I never saw one carrying one—I assume their innate toughness keeps them impervious to the elements). But you will frequently see them carrying a lunch bucket or small cooler.

In the case of female Daily Doublers, suits are often accessorized with white terry socks and running shoes. These are the true Daily Doubler women, having learned from acquiring broken shoe heels when running over pavement to make up time from a behind-schedule train, that there is no need to torture one's feet with high heels until they actually arrive at their places of work. When it comes to making an impression with expensive footwear, the train ride does not count.

Accoutrements

Initially I thought to call this section "Luggage" but chose not to, because a real Daily Doubler is not usually carrying anything that amounts to actual luggage. Luggage is for airplanes and hotels, not the bare minimum of items that a typical Daily Doubler carries on the train. And besides, the three A's had a nice ring to it, whereas the "2 A's and 1L" is not very catchy.

Through careful planning and the experience that comes from making this trip for what seemed like a zillion times, Daily Doublers have learned to walk the fine line between bringing only what is necessary and carrying enough provisions to personally lead a group of mountaineers up Mount Everest. So they keep it simple:

1. Book or newspaper
2. Umbrella
3. Laptop. This is great for getting work done and squeezing a few drops of productivity out of this generally useless part of your workday (or watching movies, as I have witnessed a few times)
4. iPod or other music-producing device. High-tech cell phones or smart phones can be invaluable here by combining several functions in one small, light-weight

component to carry; many Daily Doublers get the latest and greatest cell phones available for this reason

5. Briefcase (or helmet, for construction workers)

Attitude

As I said, Daily Doublers do not normally fritter away their time with idle conversation with their seatmates. They are not there to make friends, they are focused on a single objective: get to work. They mostly focus on their book, newspaper, laptop, etc., except for brief, pointed glances at schedules and signage, and furtive glances to either side (people-watching, of course.) They are not unfriendly most of the time. However, their politeness exhibits itself more in making themselves as innocuous as possible to fellow Daily Doublers, to allow everyone to ride the train without their space encroached upon or their routines disturbed, than in showing a broad smile to every passerby. They are all business, on automatic, and woe betide those who interrupt this part of their day with a question or an inane attempt at conversation. They will politely answer your question, but the reality is, they don't really want to be bothered with a moderately pleasant, superficial give-and-take about the weather or the Yankees or the economy. They do this every day, darn it, leave them alone!

It took me a while to come up with my own personalized routine for my 90-minute train ride. Prior to joining the Daily Doubler community, my train rides were infrequent. I could easily pass the time just looking out the window and musing at the changes in scenery as we rattled through suburbs and cities. Once I started riding the train daily, looking out the window became boring very quickly. Nothing changes. I needed something different, a routine that would help pass the time, make the trip more tolerable.

For me, that was best accomplished by sleeping. Having always been a fan of the nap, after perfecting this art during long family car rides over the years, this was a no-brainer for me. I became accomplished at finding a comfortable position, closing my eyes, and falling asleep. I was able to enhance this experience by adding a musical component to induce slumber. I would put my earphones on, select the music feature on my cell phone, slide into my comfort zone and I was out, fast! Two naps a day? Are you kidding? I felt like a college kid all over again.

Unfortunately, I soon realized from hard experience that there is one big risk with using sleep as your main pastime for the train ride. *It is very important that you wake up in time to exit the train when it reaches your destination.* This is not a concern if your destination is the last stop that the train makes, as was the case for my morning commute. The train ride ended at Grand Central Station. The train would stop, I would be jolted awake, and de-board the train with everyone else. With this built-in alarm, sleeping all the way to Grand Central was not a problem.

My commute home, however, was another issue. I won't bore you with the embarrassing details. Just trust me when I tell you that waking up suddenly from a deep sleep, confused and wondering what instinct suddenly wrenched you from the depths of slumber, then looking out and seeing the name of your town flash by your eyes as the train leaves your station is not a pleasant experience.

There is another group that makes up a small subset of the Daily Doubler that should not be overlooked. These are students, probably high school students who attend schools in towns other than where they live. Students fall into this category because they see themselves as daily commuters, although they obviously don't ride the train during summer vacations or other school breaks.

The 3 A's for student Daily Doublers (or Junior Doublers or Mini Doublers, I leave that to you) are, as follows:

Attire

Some of the private schools in my area require students to be dressed in uniform or follow a strict dress code. However, I was struck by the creativity of students who, when faced with such a rigid rule, could concoct outfits that walked the very line of breaking the rules of their dress codes. Girls accessorized their staid navy blue jumpers with a rainbow of turtlenecks, oxford shirts, patterned leggings, and even sweatpants. And as for the young men...well, I never saw such a variety of unique neckties, lolling loosely around the collars of their wearers until the last moment before the train hit the school station, when it seemed a spell would fall over the crowd and there was a rush to tighten, straighten, and smooth for inspection.

Students that attended public schools did not have the same rigid dress codes. Given the freedom to wear pretty much anything they wanted, it was very easy to determine those students from the private school ones. Jeans, un-tucked shirts, sneakers, and baseball caps (usually worn lop-sided) were common among the males. The young ladies favored jeans also (although at times these were replaced with skirts), often combined with blouses, sweaters, jackets, and scarves in many more colorful shades and interesting patterns than their elder Daily Doubler counterparts.

Accoutrements

The typical Daily Doubler (student version) would carry a book bag, usually a backpack, which would not be carried in the way that backpacks are meant to be carried so they do their job and distribute weight evenly on one's back. Backpacks were invariably slung casually over one shoulder, which I am sure produced a yearly crop of new patients for the chiropractic community of Fairfield County, CT.

In addition to these backpacks, students frequently have more carry-on equipment with them than the adult traveler. For with school comes class projects, after-school activities, and with activities comes equipment. I have seen everything from guitars to lacrosse sticks carried by these young commuters. If one of them ever got on the train pulling a hand-truck with an upright piano on it, I would not have been surprised.

Attitude

Although some students liked to exhibit the world-weary nonchalance of the Daily Doubler, trying to acquit themselves as seasoned travelers for whom a train ride was no big deal, most students don't tend to be as quiet as the adult Daily Doubler. This can be explained by their youthful exuberance. Hey, we were all young once, right? You will see them on their phones, talking with their friends about the big game last night or gossiping about the latest romance or breakup to hit the schoolyard, or singing to their music, while listening with their headphones on. You may even catch a glimpse of a young couple in love listening to the same song, sharing the earphones, one using the left, the other using the right. Why is it that the only ones you ever hear singing like that are <u>not</u> the ones in the choir?

The final, and somewhat bittersweet, distinguishing factor for students is the frequency of turnover in this group. As students get older, other means of transportation become available. It's my guess the most popular is driving their own automobile or catching a ride with buddy who was fortunate enough to have their sixteenth birthday within the confines of the current school year. As the older students leave the train for the comfort of their, or their friend's cars, they are replaced by a new crop of younger ones. And the cycle continues. One good use for people-watching is to observe how the students change as they progress through this cycle. Students that are new to the train commute are quiet as they try to find their way and establish themselves as a Daily Doubler. As the older ones leave the train commute, the younger students are promoted to the senior ranks and begin to be much more vocal and popular.

It used to make me think about life—how the young are always moving onward and upward to the next thing, gaining a foothold on the next rung in the ladder. We always wanted to grow up, get to the next life phase that signified our adulthood. When did I hit the point where I wanted to be back in their shoes? And what does it mean that I ended up right alongside them on the train, witnessing their journey and thinking of my own?

Note: the Local Daily Doubler: there's an exception to every rule

Now, before all you Daily Doublers sit up, stop reading, and protest my generalizations, let me clarify. Yes, there are some exceptions to the rule. I didn't forget you: it's true that local commuters tend to be to be more talkative than their long distance brethren. This was something I did not realize early on in my commutation days.

During my commute to New York, the train that I often rode had 3 stops after mine, the last being in Fairfield, Connecticut. From that stop, it was an express to Grand Central Station. Every rider on that train was heading to New York and had a long ride ahead of them. They were true Daily Doublers as defined above. This worked perfectly for me. After boarding the train, I would read my newspaper, usually completing by the time we arrived in Fairfield. Knowing that the train would run non-stop from that point on, it was perfect time for me to settle in for a satisfactory nap.

After enduring, I mean, enjoying, this commute for several months, I was assigned to work on a project for a client in Stamford, CT for several months. Since the train I was accustomed to riding did not stop in Stamford, I was forced to find another. The one I chose only had 2 stops after I boarded, the last being in Bridgeport, before it ran express to Stamford. Although this shortened my time for reading my newspaper, I was able to do so by the time we reached Bridgeport. This left me with enough time for a short nap before arriving in Stamford. But what I never realized was the difference in the atmosphere on this train, and even more so on the train ride home.

At the end of my time in Stamford, I resumed my commute to New York. However, I had made a change to the train ride home at the end of the day. I began taking the train from New York that stopped in Stamford. This was the same train I rode home every day while working in that city. But now, I had slept from New York to Stamford, where I woke, and remained awake for the remainder of my ride to Milford. It was at this point where I realized how different these Daily Doublers were.

When they boarded the train, they brought with them much more enthusiasm than those of us who began our journey long before these commuters entered our domain. And, like the rest of us, while they had just finished a long, hard day at work, they seemed to have a renewed sense of energy. I gave this some thought and came up with a few possible reasons for this behavior.

1. the shorter commute left less time for other diversions (sleep, read, work, etc.) so they *had* to talk
2. the shorter the commute, the more likely people that live near each other and know each other work together, so a friendship already exists.
3. the shorter commute is less intrusive in their life, so they just take it for granted. Strategic planning is not as imperative as it was for those of us who were spending upwards of 3 precious hours a day on the train.
4. these people were clearly hitting the bars before they boarded the train, or sneaking liquor in their morning coffee.

But while these local commuters exhibit some dissimilar tendencies than the long distance commuters, they can still be considered Daily Doublers. They ride the rails every day, back and forth to work. They appreciate the value of the train service. Although they did display more excitement, they were courteous to the other Daily Doublers, keeping their conversations relatively low.

Should you have the opportunity to ride the train during the peak hours, when most of the Daily Doublers are doing so, be courteous, follow the tips on etiquette. You can be sure *they* will. In the end, the ride will be more enjoyable for everyone.

7. Day Tripper

"Day Trippers" are infrequent train riders that take the train to their destination for a specific purpose on a specific day. You probably know the Day Trippers by their more well-known designation, "tourists". For example, a Day Tripper may take the train into New York to see a show, have dinner, attend a sporting event or just sightsee. They are not going to work, they are experiencing an event. The train ride is part of that event, if not the most important. A poor start to a trip could lead to angry children, mothers or fathers and overshadow the excitement of the whole event. A fun train ride is all very well and good for *them*, but it makes for some annoying interactions with Daily Doublers, who mostly see the train as a means to an end, an experience to be endured rather than savored.

Because they do not ride the rails regularly, they may not be aware of the tips on etiquette, and therefore, will probably not follow them. Hopefully, they do follow some basic rules of polite human conduct. But even this may be too much to expect, as some of my observations may suggest.

Unlike the Daily Doubler whose trip is routine and mundane, the Day Tripper is not going to work. They are on an excursion. There is excitement. They see the ride as part of that and their excitement often is very apparent.

Attire:

Naturally, the Day Tripper's attire would be dependent on what takes them into the city. The wide variety of wardrobe made my people-watching exercise more challenging as I attempted to guess where they might be headed for the day. Of course, in most cases, I never really knew the answer. To do so would mean taking the day off and following a Day Tripper through the city, and while that would make for a more fun and interesting experience than my typical day at the office, it would not pay the bills. And what would I say later that evening at the dinner table when Corinne asked me about my day?

In the early hours of the morning, when most Daily Doublers are suited up for work, Day Trippers distinguish themselves in shorts and golf shirts, sneakers or comfortable sandals, sometimes even a sun hat. Destination: Bronx Zoo. Suburban women headed in for a day of Christmas shopping and Rockefeller Center tree-viewing might be dressed in jeans and shoes comfortable enough for walking, with a puffy coat to stay warm while wandering the streets of New York laden with packages, in search of a picturesque place for lunch or a cup of hot cocoa. In the evening, Day Trippers may even appear in casual clothing, maybe carrying a small suitcase. I reasoned these folks might be headed for dinner and a Broadway show, followed by an overnight stay in a local hotel.

Accoutrements:

Day Trippers, on average, have more bags with them when compared to the Daily Doubler. Even if this is not true on their trip *to* their destination, it is almost always the case on the way *back*. Shopping and sightseeing offer an array of opportunities to buy things, so it is not uncommon to see Day Trippers headed home with several bags, some very large. These carryons take up valuable space on the train. Trains have limited storage space, and when you're taking public transportation, you might want to take the comfort of others into consideration before you decide to load up with the entire contents of FAO Schwarz. My guess is they feel obliged to buy a gift for everyone who could not join them for the day, or perhaps Day Trippers feel it is their personal mission to support our national economy. God Bless America and God Bless Day Trippers!

Another accoutrement of the typical Day Tripper is...well, more Day Trippers. They tend to run in packs, and, enclosed within their small group, are frequently oblivious to others riding the train. Quite often they are young people and families. Anticipation, coffee, and snacks fuel their energy on the way to their destination. Conversation is non-stop. Young adults may listen to their iPod while moms and dads may read a story to their young children to keep them from running up and down the aisles. On their return trip, Day Trippers are typically less energetic, succumbing to the events of the day. Their exhaustion is evident. Kids are often restless and whiny, even crying as their parents try to calm them down and get them to sleep. Daily Doublers can be easily annoyed with their noise and antics, but they recognize them as inexperienced train travelers and try to simply accept or ignore their behavior. The experienced Daily Doubler has honed his/her skills to the point that they can easily tune out these distractions and focus on their own routine. There are however, a few characteristics that the Day Trippers may exhibit that can be very agitating to the Daily Doubler. Storing their packages on a seat, which prevents a Daily Doubler from sitting, can be irritating. And we can do without the ongoing strolling up and down the aisle to visit with friends who were forced to sit apart after making the trip together.

Attitude:

Now you may be expecting me to criticize Day Trippers, assuming their attitude says, "Hey, this is my day, my event, I don't really care about the rest of you." Well, you're wrong. I don't see Day Trippers as selfish; I see them more as unaware. They're excited, ready to have fun and make the most of their day in the city. Since they don't travel by train as frequently as the Daily Doubler, they don't recognize there is a difference in their approach to the train ride. They probably feel they are one and the same. However, they are not.

One tendency that quickly betrays the presence of a tourist is the use of cell phones. We'll discuss cell phones later in the etiquette chapter, but briefly, the rules regarding cell phone usage is, DON'T! Of course there are exceptions, like when you know you're going to be late to work/home/a meeting/an airline flight and you need to contact your boss/wife/client/travel agent and let them know, but generally speaking, cell phone usage should be kept to a minimum. If it is necessary to use your phone, you should talk quietly and keep the call short.

Even Daily Doublers often have a need to use their cell phone while on the train, but it is much different from the type of call that is often placed by a Day Tripper who wants to share their excitement with friends and family at home:

"Is Gloria there? Yeah, put her on. How are you, by the way? Yeah, on my way home now. What a day! Lemme tell you, New York ain't all it's cracked up

to be. Used to be...oh, hi, Gloria. Well, I was just telling Irv that New York ain't what it used to be. Remember when we used to go as kids? Wait a sec. Can you hear me better now? Well, I have to shout because this darn train is so loud. No, it was a nice day. Shouldn't complain, better than working, right? Yeah...Yeah....Yeah, we went to the Met. Not the opera, silly, can you imagine me at the opera? No, the museum.....".

Listening to one side of a conversation where people are loudly rehashing their day can be one of the most annoying things one can experience. This is especially true at the end of a long day at work.

Another issue that can cause friction between Daily Doublers and Day Trippers is slowness. Now, I know that life is a journey and we are supposed to stop and smell the roses once in a while. I'm the last person who wants to spoil someone's vacation day. But please, if you're not headed to the place where you need the vacation *from*, then step aside and let me get through!

Now that you have a feel for the differences between Daily Doublers and Day Trippers, I want to share with you a few experiences I have witnessed as the two worlds collide.

The first has to do with purchasing the train ticket. There may be several ways to purchase a train ticket. For example, on Metro North, you can buy them online, at a kiosk located on the platform (if available), or from the conductor on the train. Most Daily Doublers buy a monthly pass online. This is simple and most cost-effective for those of us who were riding every day. But Day Trippers would have no reason to do this for one trip, so they often buy their ticket using the kiosk. Watching them do so can be fun, unless you are a Daily Doubler who forgot your monthly pass and are now standing in line behind this newcomer (OK, yes, it happened to me), in which case it can drive you into that state that previews an impending apoplectic fit.

First, they have to parade through the whole process screen after screen, because they are unfamiliar with the steps and must read and consider each one carefully before making their selection:

Where am I boarding the train?
What's my destination?
Do I want a Metro card for the subway too?
How many tickets do I want?
How old am I?
Am I traveling during peak hours?

Do I want a receipt?

Will I pay with cash, debit or credit card?

So many questions to answer, all while others are anxiously waiting their turn in line, wondering what is taking so long. The tension mounts as the horn of the train blasts, far off in the distance, signaling it is rapidly closing in on your station. Your hands tremble and all you can think of is this: *If I buy my ticket on the train, there is an extra charge!*

Finally, the person is done hitting all the right buttons and the ticket prints out. All that is left is to get their change. Now, if you ever wondered where all those one-dollar coins went, I am convinced the railroad has all of them. Because all your change is in coins, even the dollars. Good luck trying to use them anywhere else--the cashiers at the grocery store have never seen them before and tend to think you are trying to pay with Skeeball tokens.

And so, much of the annoyance that a Daily Doubler feels around a Day Tripper can be caused by their lack of familiarity with the whole process, but some of that irritation is probably just plain envy. After all, we've long lost sight of the fun of a train ride. We do it every day, and we're not going to the Bronx Zoo or Rockefeller Center—we're going to work. The excitement is over and we are left with a daily routine and commute that seems more grueling by the day.

Another experience I witnessed was actually very exciting. On one cold February morning in 2008, the train ride into Manhattan, normally dominated by Daily Doublers, was overrun with Day Trippers, all with a common cause. You see, that day there was a parade up Broadway, through the Canyon Of Heroes in honor of the Superbowl Champions, The New York Giants. Day Trippers were out in force, growing in numbers at each stop along the way and packing the train cars with a herd of fans dressed in Giants shirts, hats, gloves, you name it. Daily Doublers were soon overcome by a sea of blue (Giants blue!), but they didn't seem annoyed in any way. The energy and excitement brought on by the Day Trippers brought a refreshing air for the rest of us who had become accustomed to our mundane ride every day...for that morning, we were all Giants fans, carried away with excitement.

On another occasion, my sister-in-law and her husband had come to visit us for a few days. During their stay, they wanted to go to New York for a day, to visit Ground-Zero and Wall Street. By now I was very familiar with area, having worked there for over a year. So when my dear wife requested I take a day off and show them around, I agreed. You can imagine how excited I was to take a day off (a very rare opportunity) and then have to spend it chaperoning others to the exact same location I commuted every day. Yes, the same train and subway ride. We even got so close to my office that when asked where I worked, I simply pointed at the window on the 16th floor. Some day off!

As for the my guests, they were all, of course Day Trippers. And I had been a Daily Doubler for a long time at that point. But traveling with these vacationers, I was perplexed. Do I behave as a Daily Doubler or a Day Tripper? I did not want to take away from their excitement. And besides, it was exciting for me. Rather than the typical mundane daily routine of commute, work, and commute, I was on vacation too. I had the opportunity to actually roam the areas of New York that I simply passed by on my way to work every day and now be able to really take it all in. Thus, for that day, I became a Day Tripper. So while the two sisters sat together and chatted for the duration of the train ride into the city, so did Jim and I. I now understood how Day Trippers see the train ride: instead of an ordeal to get through, it's part of the fun and an energizing start to an exciting day.

So the lesson to be learned is that Daily Doublers and Day Trippers can get along.

Finally, because Day Trippers are seldom riders of the rails, they are not aware of many of the tips that will be presented later in this book. Daily Doublers can use their experience to get an advantage over the Day Tripper when selecting the right car and seat. The Day Tripper does not really care much about which side of the train they sit on or whether they sit in the same well chosen spot every day, their only real desire is to get seats that are together so they can remain as a group.

But heaven help the Day Tripper who sits in a Daily Doubler's normal seat!

8. Stealth Rider

The third category I like to call the Stealth Rider. I like how it sounds. Stealth technology is used to confuse and deceive the enemy, and very often, Stealth Riders confuse and deceive Daily Doublers. The Stealth Rider is similar to the Daily Doubler in that this person travels by train for a business-related reason, such as to attend a meeting or seminar or visit a client. However, unlike the Daily Doubler, the train trips are infrequent. As a result, he/she exhibits some of the same characteristics of the Day Tripper. In this way, the Stealth Rider looks like the Daily Doubler, but often behaves like the Day Tripper.

The 3 A's for Stealth Riders are:

Attire:

Stealth Riders typically travel alone, during peak hours of the work week, the same time as the Daily Doublers. This is the first aspect of the Stealth Rider that makes it difficult to identify them. Their dress is the same as the Daily Doublers, allowing them to blend in. A Daily Doubler might allow a Stealth Rider to take the seat next to them, breathing a sigh of relief that it's one of their kind.

Only when they exhibit Day Tripper traits do they stand out, betraying their unfamiliarity with standard Daily Doubler practices and alerting us to their true identity as a Stealth Rider.

Accoutrements:

There is another simple way to spot them. If you see a person with no tools to pass the time such as a book or magazine, and staring out the window with a look of true curiosity, that's probably a Stealth Rider. Stealth Riders can often be easily spotted by what they don't, rather than what they do, carry with them. If they have a laptop, they don't generally take it out, preferring instead to look out the window, viewing the train ride as a bonus of free time where work need not be accomplished. After all, they're off site for the day. Perhaps they need to calm their nerves at this extra piece of stress that the train ride is adding to an already stressful day of negotiating the city and getting through whatever meeting or conference they will be attending.

Before I began traveling to New York on a daily basis, I would do so periodically for business reasons. I was a Stealth Rider, although I did not know it at the time. Fortunately, understanding basic etiquette, I did not exhibit many of the Day Tripper characteristics. But the one I did show was staring out the window. It was almost hypnotic. My moments of nervousness also betrayed me as a Stealth Rider. Not being used to a routine train ride, I was constantly checking my pockets for all the essentials, afraid that I lost something and would be stranded in the city, gone forever, never to see my loved ones again. I would check for my money and credit cards, identification, train ticket, subway metrocard, receipts, car keys, pocket train schedule, breath mints repeatedly during the train ride. I carried so much in my pockets I had no worry of being blown away by the strong winds that whistle through the streets of New York.

Over time, as a Stealth Rider travels by train more and more, he/she will eventually move into the Daily Doubler category. This occurs when boredom sets in and the trip becomes more routine. But it does take time, and a seasoned Daily Doubler can usually tell the difference. Once I became a full-fledged Daily Doubler, I understood what that meant regarding my behavior on the train. Then it happened. I, a Daily Doubler was matched with a Stealth Rider. Now this may not seem like such a big deal, but for a Daily Doubler, it can be an agonizing experience, as you will see.

Attitude:

The major difference between the attitudes of Daily Doublers and Stealth Riders can best be illustrated with an experience I had. My brother Andy, a professional businessman in his own right, had a meeting in New York. With my familiarity of Grand Central Station and the subway system, we decided to ride together. I thought this would be an ideal situation, one where two like-minded individuals could enjoy a smooth traveling experience. Read: I thought he would let me nap.

See, Andy has lived and worked in many places, from a small, slow-paced town in Wisconsin, to the crowded, fast-paced southeast coast of Florida, with some time in Pennsylvania, New York, Connecticut and even Germany. The nature of his line of work caused him to travel a lot (although none of it was by train, as I was later to find out). Thus, I was expecting him to understand the rules of train travel for a well-traveled businessman.

Boy, was I in for a surprise. When we boarded the train, we settled into seats that faced each other. That was violation number one, as you will see in the section on seat selection later in this book. The second violation soon became apparent. He wanted to talk all the way! Instead of a quiet ride with another businessman, I was subjected to non-stop conversation from my brother. ARGH!!! In the interest of maintaining the family bond, I had to appear courteous and interested, but I was also a Daily Doubler. Unlike my day as a Day Tripper with my inlaws, it was not as simple as just taking on the personality of a Stealth Rider. It was easy to put on the Day Tripper attitude and step into vacation mode for a day. I had different companions, a day off from work, even different clothes. But heading to work alongside a Stealh Rider was different from the start. I was hyper-aware of the fact that, as an established Daily Doubler, I had responsibilities to fulfill, an attitude to portray. Choosing to maintain family harmony, I bowed to his desire for conversation, but suffered great internal strife at my divided loyalties.

A few stops later, as the train began to fill up, two other people joined us in our little cove. One would think that having a few strangers enter into our private world would signal the end of conversation and I could settle into my daily commuting routine, my nap. WRONG again! We continued our conversation for the remainder of our trip. Needless to say, this disruption to my normal routine affected my entire day. Rather than being refreshed and ready to get working when I arrived at my office, I was dragging and not looking forward to the day ahead. But he was my brother, what could I do? As children growing up, we had the typical brother-love relationship. We had our battles and disagreements. As the older brother, tormenting my younger brother was a responsibility I took seriously. Besides, with three other siblings, if we were not battling, someone else probably was. Looking back now, it's nice to know we all survived. Today, we are all very close, so I guess riding together and catching up on stories of our own children was not so bad after all.

My advice to Daily Doublers? If you must travel with a Stealth Rider, brief him on the rules and expectations. He may feel taken aback at first, but you must protect your own sanity and, most importantly, your reputation on the train. Remember, the next day he will be gone and you will be alone again with your fellow Daily Doublers.

There you have it. Are you a Daily Doubler, Day Tripper, or Stealth Rider? Or maybe you have another category for your type of rider that does not fit in any of these three. Regardless of the rider type you are, the next chapters will help you as you prepare for your future train rides, beginning with a discussion on basic etiquette. I am a big believer that proper etiquette should always be practiced at all times, even more so when people are stuffed together in an enclosed environment. It is one tactic for ensuring that all types of riders can travel together comfortably, without insult or incident.

9. First, You Address The Ball

Many of you will remember the old black and white television show, *The Honeymooners*. If you don't, then I've just made myself feel even older than I did when I mentioned *Casablanca!* But that's another topic entirely, and not one I want to talk about right now. Anyway, this classic of American television starred Jackie Gleason as Ralph Kramden, and Art Carney as his best friend, Ed Norton. It was popular in the good 'ol days when your television only got three channels and you watched whatever your parents wanted to watch. As you can imagine, my parents, along with many others, watched *The Honeymooners*, so I got to like it real fast. In one of my favorite episodes, Ed was explaining golf to Ralph. He told Ralph, "First, you address the ball... hello, ball".

Makes sense, right? Pretty simple? Sure seems so. Well, actually, no, it isn't. In golf, addressing the ball is not like addressing another person. If you were to address the ball in this way, you would not only be wrong, you would get quite a lot of strange looks from your fellow golfers. Addressing the ball is the first step in the game of golf, and it means to place the ball in the proper position for play, or to position yourself if the ball is already in play, in order to take your next swing. So when I see someone take something that is so basic and simple and get it wrong, I think of this famous line.

This is how I look at basic etiquette. Webster defines etiquette as *"the conduct or procedure required by good breeding or prescribed by authority to be observed in social or official life"*.[3] Wikipedia defines etiquette as *"a code that influences expectations for social behavior according to contemporary conventional norms within a society, social class, or group"*.[4] My parents defined it as *"remember, you're a Macdonald, act like it!"* It seems like an easy thing to practice, and if everyone follows the rules, life will run much more smoothly, free of conflict.

---

[3] Merriam-Webster's Collegiate Dictionary Tenth Edition
[4] http://en.wikipedia.org/wiki/Etiquette

I like to think that etiquette is one of the things that separate mankind from all other life forms. In fact, people that don't practice proper etiquette are often referred to as animals. When practiced properly, it's what allows perfect strangers to interact without incident (we hope). Different cultures may have different standards of behavior but there are many universal forms too, such as "please and thank you." The trouble comes when people are unaware of the rules of etiquette and decide to make things up as they go along.

Individual activities have their own rules of etiquette. To carry forward with our golf example for a moment (I'll get to trains soon, not to worry), practicing proper etiquette is considered an important part of the game. Not only is it expected, failure to do so can even affect the outcome of a game. Being quiet when a golfer is hitting the ball, replacing divots, keeping a steady pace of play...these are just a few of the rules that make up golf etiquette.

The worst violation of golf etiquette that I ever witnessed occurred a number of years ago. My buddy George and I were playing golf on a beautiful afternoon. The sky was blue, a slight breeze with the fresh smell of spring was in the air. Being on a golf course was the best place to be. Directly ahead of us was a man playing golf, alone.

Now normally, two players following one should not be a problem. With only one golfer in front of you, you'll usually find that he speeds ahead after a time, or, if he likes to take his time, he'll allow you to "play through," that is, ask you to pass him and continue on your merry way. This golfer, unfortunately, was unaware of the rules of golf etiquette. Every time he prepared to hit his ball, he performed the following routine:

- Set golf bag on the ground
- Remove his sweater
- Select a club
- Take a few practice swings
- Return the club to the bag, select another club
- Take a few more practice swings
- Hit the ball
- Return the club to the bag
- Put his sweater back on

Pick up his bag and walk to the ball and begin the process all over again

Needless to say, play for us and everyone behind us slowed, and tensions began to flare. It was obvious this person did not understand one of the basic tenets of etiquette on the golf course: keep moving. I was not close enough to hear him (or grab him by his sweater and physically set him aside so the rest of us could play through, a thought which did enter my mind after a while) but I am positive that if I were closer, I would have heard him say "hello, ball" each time he prepared to hit it.

With larger groups of people, practicing proper etiquette can help prevent problems. This is very true when people are crowded into a train for a lengthy ride. This is even more important when there are not enough seats for everyone, forcing some to stand. And when the train is comprised of a mix of Daily Doublers, Day Trippers and Stealth Riders, proper etiquette carries even more significance.

Below is a list of suggested tips for how to behave on the train. This is not an exhaustive list but covers many common actions. Once you read them, you will probably think they are just a matter of "common sense." In all cases, if you follow this simple rule of thumb, you will be fine: be considerate and respectful of others.

Suggestion #1: Boarding The Train

If you are waiting to board the train, it follows that the train will need to empty before you can get on and find a seat. Right? If you have a big box of rocks and you want to replace the rocks in the box with other rocks, what do you do first? *Take out the excess rocks.* The train works on the same principle. Let people exiting the train, EXIT THE TRAIN! How hard is that? Think about it, later, when YOU want to get off, don't YOU get upset when people boarding rush in before YOU can get out? Let them out! Don't worry, you will get on. The train won't leave without you.

Suggestion #2: Ticket Readiness

Have your ticket ready for the conductor. These people are good at this. They can zip through a train car in minutes if the passengers are ready. And the sooner they do, the sooner you can settle into your routine. It's okay to chat briefly with the conductor, but remember they have a job to do and others are waiting. Really, you bought the ticket in order to get on the train, are you so surprised they are taking tickets that you must become completely flustered when the conductor arrives at your seat, then proceed to explain that you know it's in there somewhere as you rifle through your pockets and bags for this small piece of paper, only to find it wedged among other small pieces of paper 15 minutes later? The conductor isn't going to use the powers of ESP to determine whether you have the right to be on this train or not, so have your ticket ready!

Suggestion #3: Store Luggage Properly

Unlike airplanes, trains place no limit on how much luggage its travelers can bring on board. However, please understand that there is limited storage room available in a train. Your luggage should be stored in the overhead racks, if available, or on your lap. Do not put it on an empty seat if someone wishes to sit there. If there is an empty seat between you and another passenger and no one needing a seat, it's ok to use the middle seat to store a bag or other item, but be willing to share the spare seat with your fellow passenger. And, ALWAYS, keep your stuff from touching other riders.

Suggestion #4: Conversation

If traveling with another or in a group, talk quietly; sit next to each other if possible. In many cases, if a stranger is sitting between you and your friend, the stranger will offer to switch seats. But in the event he/she does not, it is acceptable to ask him/her to do so. If you do so politely and they are not already settled in, they will probably comply, rather than have to sit between you and your companion, which would expose them to more of your conversation than they wish to hear. Trust me, no one wants to know what is going on in your life.

Suggestion #5: Cell phone

In today's society, it is common for everyone to have his or her own cell phones. It seems that many of us cannot be without them. They have become a way of life. It may be understandable that people must use their cell phones while on the train, but please try to keep your conversations short and speak quietly. Often times you will hear the conductor make an announcement requesting the same and to move to the vestibule if you must talk at length. And please, PLEASE put the ringer on vibrate, to avoid the symphony of intermittent cell phone rings followed by the united knee-jerk reaction of heads turning and hands going to pockets. After all, Mozart was never meant to be interpreted into a series of beeps.

Suggestion #6: Pay Attention to Your Children

We all know how hard it is to keep young children under control at times. I've raised two very active boys, so I definitely do understand! Kids are easily excitable and riding on a train can increase this excitement for many children. But it is the responsibility of the parents or guardians of the children to keep them under control so as not to disturb other riders. Babies cry, we all know that. When it happens there's little you can do about it, it's okay. The same is not true for young children. They may act up, but there *is* usually something you can do about it. Sorry, you may be tired yourself from a long day in the city, but imagine how your child feels, and pay some attention to them.

One of the worst experiences I had was on a trip home from work at the end of the day. A young mother and her daughter were seated in the row in front of me, obviously returning from a day in the city. They were Day Trippers. The little girl soon began to feel the effects of her exciting but exhausting day. Now any parent knows how a tired child can behave—they don't go blissfully to sleep, as adults do when we are tired. This girl cried and complained all the way home. But instead of trying to keep her daughter entertained and calm, the mother spent the entire trip on her cell phone, telling someone on the other end the events of their day, in detail! Listening to the ignored child cry, combined with an hour and a half long cell phone conversation, made this trip home most unbearable.

Aside from basic courtesy, it's important that you pay attention to your children so they are safe on the train. This is still a public venue, full of strangers. It's also moving at a pretty good clip, then stopping and starting with a jolt that can send a full-grown man stumbling if he's not ready for it. Letting your kids run wild up and down the aisles on a train can only produce lost, scared kids, bumped heads, and general panic and high-pitched wailing at a time when everyone would rather be winding down from a long day in relative quiet.

Suggestion #7: Music

When listening to music, use headphones and keep volume low. The purpose of headphones is so that only YOUR ears hear the music. No one else wants to hear your music. I have actually heard another person's music, emanating from their headphones, through the music playing on my own headphones! Imagine how loud that music must have been. If you want to make yourself deaf, that is your prerogative, but please, don't do it on the train.

Also, if you plan to listen to music, please, PLEASE do not sing! You know you're in public, right? Are you expecting to be discovered by a talent agent sitting across the aisle from you? Is this your audition for *American Idol*? Save your singing for the shower, like the rest of us!

Suggestion #8: Give Up Your Seat

At the root of basic etiquette is a desire for us to develop the habits of kindness and care. They're not just silly rules, they are there for a reason. Be kind, give up your seat for a disabled, pregnant, or elderly person. (Although, as an aside, it's an act of self-preservation not to mention that the reason you are giving up your seat is that you see that she is expecting a happy event. Even if you are 99% sure a woman is pregnant, do not EVER refer to that unless she mentions it herself, or goes into labor right in front of your eyes. It's good etiquette to give up your seat, not to make the mistake of assuming someone is pregnant when she is....um...not. This has never happened to me, I swear.)

Suggestion #9: Offer To Help

Offers of assistance are always welcome. If you see someone struggling to store their baggage in the overhead racks, don't sit and watch, offer to help. You will be amazed how appreciative they will be and how good you will feel.

Suggestion #10: Trash

Take it with you and discard in a trash can. Don't leave it on or stuff it under a seat. This includes newspapers. Don't worry, you won't be carrying your empty coffee cup or banana peel with you all day. The train station is full of trash cans, as are most city sidewalks that you will be walking. Nothing is more irritating than an empty can or bottle rolling back and forth under your seat, bouncing off your feet.

Suggestion #11: Hygiene

Take care of it at home. This goes for men *and* women...guys, don't think you're off the hook because you don't have a tube of lipstick and a compact mirror in your briefcase. I have seen women doing an entire makeover in their seat, using their reflection in the window as a guide. When she boarded the train, she looked like she'd just rolled out of bed, when she exited, she looked like she was ready to go on stage. But this public grooming is not an exclusively female habit–I have also seen men clipping their nails and shaving with electric shavers. Listen closely please, set your alarm 10 minutes earlier and take care of this stuff at home!

Suggestion # 12: Get A Room

Do you really need me to explain this one?

When I see a train rider violate any of these basic tips, I look at them and picture them on the golf course, standing over their ball, looking down at it and saying "Hello ball" as I pound my head with my fists.

10. Creatures Of Habit vs. Power Of Choice

My family was the typical middle-class American family of the 60's and 70's. My father worked his entire life at the Waterbury Buckle Company. He started working there right out of high school, bypassing college and moving through the ranks to retire as a Vice President. That's what you did in those days. You worked in one place your whole career, starting at the bottom and working your way up. My mother was a Registered Nurse and worked as the town's Visiting Nurse and as the school nurse at St. Thomas Catholic School. I was one of 5 children with 2 brothers and 2 sisters. And, like many similar families at that time, we always had a dog.

First there was Twiggy the Cocker Spaniel, then Missy the Beagle, followed by Pepper (1), and then Pepper (2) and Blacky at the same time. Both Peppers and Blacky were a mix of German Shepherd, Collie, and Norwegian Elkhound. Now any child with a dog knows how easy it is to train a dog to sit and raise his paw for a treat. In our case, we used cookies. Nowadays I cringe when I try to imagine the weekly grocery bill with five kids and a dog that was trained with cookies...we could have fed a small village in China with our cookie consumption alone.

Why was it so easy to train a dog this way? Because dogs are creatures of habit. They have no power of choice. You will never see a dog say "nah, I don't feel like a Snausage right now, maybe later."

Back in those days, neighborhoods were different than today, and so were neighborhood children. We did not have Play Station 3 or XBOX 360. We played outside. If we were inside, it wasn't long before our mother sent us outside again, because five kids plus the dog in one house usually added up to one big headache for her.

Riding bikes was our mode of transportation and we played whatever sport was in season at that time of year. Baseball, football, basketball, whoever had the best yard, that's where we played. We played Hide and Seek, Red Light/Green Light, Tag, and Simon Says. There were no boundaries, everyone's yard blended together. Our neighbor's yard was just an extension of our own. The same was true for our pets. There were no invisible fences to keep your dog in your yard. They roamed freely, just as we kids did.

I remember many evenings when it was bedtime. I would stand in our driveway and call for Pepper to come home.

"Pepper, Pepper, come here Pepper, come here, boy!"

No Pepper.

"Pepper, Pepper, come Pepper, come here, boy, P-E-P-P-E-R!"

Still no Pepper.

Then my mother (who had sworn she would <u>never</u> have a German Shepherd in the house but ended up being his best friend) would come out and yell the magic word.

"COOKIE, COOKIE, COOKIE!"

All of sudden I could hear the rustle of bushes and sound of four feet rapidly galloping closer and closer. In a flash there he was, sitting in front of her, with his paw raised, begging for that darned cookie. You would have thought his name was Cookie. He was a creature of habit.

I am not sure what the guys who train circus elephants to stand on their hind legs use, but if it is a cookie it would have to be the size of a Frisbee!

It is often said that people are creatures of habit too. Given the same set of circumstances, we will do the same thing, follow the same routine, the majority of time. We derive great comfort from habit. Unlike animals, we do have the power to choose. We just choose to be creatures of habit. Go figure!

Another place you can see this clearly is at church on Sunday mornings. Inevitably, the same people sit in the same rows, same seats, every Sunday. Some sit in front, some in back. Some prefer the left, others the right and the rest in the middle. But always in the same place. I do it, myself. Once in a while I will sit on the other side of the church but when I do, it just doesn't feel right.

Think about your life, when you prepare to go to work. Whether you work days or night, weekdays or weekends, do you follow the same routine every time? I know I sure do.

Do you eat breakfast or dress first? Men, do you shave before or after you shower? Ladies, do you dry your hair before or after you dress? Whatever your routine is, is it always the same?

There are good reasons for this. For one, it helps you stay on schedule so you can be out the door and at work on time. For me, it helps me make sure I don't forget something, like my watch, or lunch, or train ticket. When I was commuting, I had to get up so early that the routine was absolutely essential to my ability to get ready appropriately and on time. I was half asleep, often getting ready in the dark so as to avoid waking Corinne. If my clothes weren't laid out, I know I would have been padding my way to the car without shoes on, wondering what I'd left behind. Something important, I think...but what was it?

Changes to your routine can be very disruptive. When my commute grew from 15 minutes to two and a half hours, it required a huge adjustment in my routine, and had an impact on my entire day and week. Just getting up that much earlier was a dramatic change. Introducing the train and subway to my commute made it even more so. Looking back, I realize that this was the reason that I struggled so much my first week, why I wanted to quit when that week ended. I did not have a routine. I was like a fish out of water.

When I was driving a mere eight miles to work, my routine was pretty simple. It went like this:

1. Wake up
2. Shave
3. Shower
4. Dress
5. Eat Breakfast, read the paper
6. Brush teeth
7. Kiss my wife and hug the kids goodbye
8. Get in my car
9. Catch 15 minutes of *Imus In The Morning* on the drive to work
10. Arrive at my place of work, park as close as I could to the building entrance
11. Walk into work with a smile (well, sometimes) and begin my day

My first day of taking the train, having no routine, went something like this:

5:00 AM: Wake up, cursing under my breath
5:08: Drag myself out of bed blindly reaching for my glasses

5:12: Shave. Cut myself twice

5:21: Stumble into the shower

5:32: What the heck am I going to wear today?

5:33: Nudge Corinne to ask if she had time to iron my blue shirt

5:34: Dodge shoe thrown at my head by Corinne, who is trying to sleep

5:42: I am now dressed, what do I do now? Breakfast, breakfast...

5:43: It's getting late, no time to make coffee

5:44: Grab laptop bag, hustle to the garage

5:45: Drive through the dark streets of my town, cursing, out loud this time

5:50: No time for Dunkin Donuts, have to stop at 7-Eleven

5:59: Arrive at train station, praying for parking spot near the station, YES! Found one

6:01: Walk to the platform, stand there, staring and wondering what the heck am I doing? I must be crazy.

6:04: Train arrives, on time

6:05: Wow, I didn't realize so many people took the train in the morning...how can I get a seat? Let me just sit next to this guy here...

6:08: What's that noise? Music? From where? That guy there, with the headphones on. He must be deaf, or will be soon. Well, I'll just look out the window awhile...

6:12: OK, I'm bored.

6:15: Still bored. Wish I'd brought a book.

6:20: zzzzzzzzzzzzzz

7:35: (JOLT, SCREECH) I'm awake! I'm awake!

7:36: Run to catch subway, get trampled by several Daily Doublers who know where they are headed while I try to get my bearings

7:41: Found directions to the subway, am I headed uptown or downtown?

7:42: Oh yeah, downtown, now where are *those* stairs?

7:43 Found them, now heading down stairs to the subway platform

7:44: Look at all these people!

7:48: Subway arrives, cram in with everyone else, standing room only

8:12: Exit the subway, climb the stairs to get outside, thinking, boy, these are a lot of stairs

8:13: Look around at the cement city and begin walk to office building

8:14: It's starting to sleet. Wish I'd brought my umbrella. Do I even own an umbrella? Make mental note to buy one

8:20: Arrive at my building, wait for elevator

8:22: Sit at my desk with a sigh, feeling like I've already worked a day and am ready to punch out and go home

8:23: Where is the men's room?

After five days of this insanity, I knew I needed to plan a new routine that would put me in my comfort zone. I spent that weekend in research and planning, and the following Monday, I was ready. I prepared to execute my new strategy. I selected what I would wear and ironed my shirt the night before. And went to bed earlier so I was well rested. These simple changes had a big impact on my routine and schedule. I had my timing down pat. I knew what time to get up, to leave my house, and be ready to step on the train when it pulled into the station. The anxiety was gone. I had now become a creature of habit, and I was darn happy to be one.

I also started to observe others as they executed their routines. Some would wait inside the train station, others would go directly to the platform. Some would chat with Patty, the nice lady that worked at the station selling coffee, pastries, and newspapers. Others watched the television to get the local news and weather. Every one of us was a creature of our own habits, and those habits helped us ease into our day, every day.

Settling into my own customs made my experience much easier for me. I knew what to do, when to do it, and where to do it. I was now ready to take the next steps. I was ready to enhance my plan, to make refinements that would make my commute more comfortable, even more enjoyable, if that was possible. "Enjoyable" and "train ride" don't really go together for a Daily Doubler, we take pride in our war stories, so let's say, more acceptable.

Another big adjustment I made was to my eating schedule. Rather than have a cup of coffee before my ride, I decided to wait until I got to my desk. For one thing, it was easier for me to sleep without the caffeine. Second, by the time I got there, I needed a cup of coffee, BAD! And third, for those days where there were delays, it was best if I had not consumed too much liquid, so I could avoid having to utilize those train restrooms. I'm glad they have them, because sometimes there is simply no choice. But given the option, I would rather not take care of such business in a closet-sized space that is jolting along at high speeds.

I continued to look for ways to make improvements. I found that relying on others habits could be helpful. During the winter months I chose to stay warm by waiting within the cozy confines of the train station. Among the waiting crowd was a lady who took the 6:57AM train. By now, I had altered my schedule to take the 7:04AM train. Every morning, at approximately 6:55AM, this lady would get up off the bench and head out the door for the train platform. As she passed by the counter she would say "have a nice day, Patty" to the lady who worked the concessions and Patty would reply "you too hon". It was like clockwork, every day. I wanted to be on the platform a few minutes early for my train, and I soon realized that this brief conversation could act as my trigger. When I heard that exchange, it was time for me to make my move.

But beware, relying on others can be risky. They may make changes to their schedule that could affect yours.

I want to mention one more rider as an example of a creature of habit on the trains. One of the most interesting commuters I observed was a middle-aged lady who was always dressed in a stylish manner. Her clothes were colorful but always tasteful. I don't recall ever seeing the same outfit twice. She had a very friendly personality, chatting with fellow Daily Doublers as well as the conductors.

It seemed this lady frequently arrived on the platform just in time to board the train, yet was always able to sit in the same seat, an aisle seat. It did not seem to matter if she was first or last to board the train. She exemplified the consummate commuter to me, someone who has been doing this for a long, long time and has developed and refined her own routine to perfection. She had her seat, her newspapers and her coffee. And by the time I awoke at Grand Central, she had already left her seat (an advantage of sitting on the aisle) and was standing in the vestibule, near the door for a quick exit. My guess, she had a long walk to her final destination. This lady was a creature of habit as much as anyone I observed during my commuting time.

In the next few chapters you will read a list of tips that I came up with as I continued to strive for the perfect train ride experience. Some of them will seem like common sense, others may be something you would never have considered. Some may help you, others may not. The length of your journey will determine how many of these tips apply to you. Whatever your own situation may be, I hope that you find them helpful and interesting. Once you decide what tips are for you and you begin to follow them each time you travel, you will find that, once again, you are a creature of habit. But remember, it was your power of choice to be so!

11. Fail To Plan, Plan To Fail

If I had a nickel for every time I heard that expression, "fail to plan, plan to fail..." well, I wouldn't have had to take a job that required a train commute, that's for sure! No matter what you intend to do, if you don't have some sort of plan, you are setting yourself up for potential failure. But simply having a plan is not a guarantee of success, you need to have the *right* plan. And believe it or not, planning for a successful train experience begins before you even set foot on the train. This chapter will provide you with a list of things you should consider as you prepare for your trip. The following chapters will have tips that you can follow as your trip progresses.

Tip # 1: Arrive Early

Remember in chapter 4, Expect The Unexpected, when we discussed things we can't control? Well, you'd be surprised at how much control over your optimal train experience you can exert by simply *arriving early*, and you would be further surprised at how many people give up this control by attempting to arrive right-on-time.

Intentionally planning to arrive just when the train arrives is very risky, akin to jumping off the top of a building in Marrakesh, in the hopes that a wagon carrying a 7-foot bale of hay is passing by to break your fall. This isn't some action movie you are starring in, this is your commute. Don't expect everything to go according to your perfectly timed arrival. It is more than probable that someday when you are rushing to catch the train you will encounter Murphy's Law, which basically says that if something can go wrong, it will. It may be in the form of an unexpected traffic jam, a crowded parking lot, or a momentary stumble on your way up the stairs. Do you really want to be late to work because of a pebble in your shoe? I don't know much about this Murphy guy, but he must have led a pretty depressing life.

Arriving early provides you with the gift of extra time to allow for the unexpected. This may seem pretty simple to you and me, but

I cannot tell you how many times I have witnessed the spectacle of people running to catch the train. Sitting comfortably in my seat, looking out the window, and watching someone try to run through the snow and ice, yelling at the conductor to hold the train, can be fun to see. But there is no guarantee the conductor will hold the train. Frankly, most of us would prefer the train stay on schedule. In fact, the bedrock of train travel is that it goes by the clock and runs on time, except in extreme cases. This is one of the key factors in its value for commuters! Do you really think such an awesome display of technology and logistics is subject to the whims of those of us who would prefer an extra four minutes of sleep to an early arrival at the train station?

Now, there are exceptions to every rule, but I highly recommend you not assume you can be that exception. The fashionable lady I introduced to you in the last chapter was one such exception. As a creature of habit, she would always arrive just minutes before the train, sometimes at the exact same time. She had clearly elevated her arrival time to an art, but I often wondered how many times she may have missed the train over the years. It seemed like a little too much living on the edge for me. Give yourself extra time, you will not regret it.

Tip #2: Pack Lightly

There is limited room on the train, especially during peak times. Be considerate of others and only bring with you what you need. In addition to laptop, backpacks, and other small carryons, I have seen travelers with suitcases, and even bicycles.

Obviously you have to pack whatever fits your needs. Whether you are a Day Tripper traveling for a short stay with friends, or a health nut that prefers a bicycle for local transportation, be thoughtful in your packing and storage during the train ride. Larger items should be placed in the vestibule of the train car, certainly not in the aisles where they will obstruct people's ability to walk through the car without mishap. Suitcases can be put in the overhead racks if room is available. However, larger luggage may take up valuable space that could be used by several other riders. It could also be downright dangerous when lifting to store and retrieve.

The most extreme example of *not* packing lightly I ever saw? One day I watched two men load up a number of boxes they were delivering to a customer in New York City. They needed a hand truck to get all the boxes on the train. The process seemed to take forever, delaying our departure and causing the train to be late arriving at the next stop. Once loaded, the boxes took up half of the storage rack on one side of the car, leaving other riders to sit with luggage and parcels in their laps for the entire ride. And why on earth would they choose such a complicated, unwieldy process for delivery? It was simply cheaper to do so this way than to ship via Federal Express, UPS or the United States Postal System.

Tip # 3: Bring Sunglasses

Despite planning to avoid sitting where the sun may be in your eyes, you should be prepared that it may happen. Over the course of a long train ride that coincides with the rising or setting of the sun, you may not have any control over the sun being in your eyes, even if you choose your seat with strategic care. Having sunglasses sure can help. Whether you are traveling during the day or at night, you should bring your sunglasses. This is because even at night, the interior lights of the train will probably be on, and if you intend to sleep during your ride, the sunglasses may come in handy. It helps. Just remember, if you travel at night, to take them off when you wake up or you will get a lot of funny looks. Trust me on that one.

Tip #4: Bring Your Desired Form of Entertainment

Unless you just plan to look out the window, people-watch, or sleep, you should bring something to help pass the time, especially if your trip is lengthy. And we have already touched on the fact that these activities, while fun at first, lose their charm in proportion to the amount of time you are forced to perform them. So choose some form of entertainment, and make sure you have it with you. You can bring a book (like this one!), magazine, newspaper, iPod, or anything else that will entertain you. You can even bring some work with you. Many Daily Doublers actually prefer to work, but I was not one of them. Most important, please avoid anything that may be disruptive or annoying to your fellow passengers.

Tip #5: Coffee and a Bite

You may want to get a cup of coffee or tea, or a bottle of orange juice for the ride. Some stations sell coffee and pastries, other stations do not. You may choose to stop on your way to the train station at Dunkin Donuts for a latté, Starbucks for a bold cup of coffee, or Panera Breads for a scone. Get whatever treat you want, but just make sure you get to the train in time. And please discard your trash in a receptacle when you arrive at your destination. Do NOT leave it on the floor of the train, this isn't a stadium and they are not going to come around with that cool little brush and dustpan thing when you leave.

Tip #6: Buy Your Ticket in Advance

While you can usually purchase your ticket on the train, you will pay much higher prices. You can also expect to get a lot of aggravated looks as you fumble to find cash to pay the conductor. Some stations may have ticket machines on the platform. You may also be able to purchase monthly and weekly tickets online, saving you time, money, and aggravation. Check your train system for alternatives to buying tickets.

Tip #7: Know Your Destination – Take The Express

Every so often someone will get on an express train, unaware that it does not stop at their destination. Once the train leaves the station, there is no going back. Know where you are heading and be sure to take a train that stops there. On the other hand, if you are lucky enough to have an express train that does stop at your destination, definitely take it. But pay attention! Often I have seen people miss their stops simply because they were not paying attention. They got on the train paying attention, they were paying attention for the first few minutes, and they were paying attention for the first several miles. Then they allowed themselves to daydream for a moment and WHAMMO! Missed stop.

Tip #8: Use the Facilities

I strongly urge you to use the restroom facilities before you begin your trip, especially if you plan to follow tip #5. No matter how short your trip may be, you must expect the unexpected. It is not unusual for a delay to occur, forcing you to sit and wait. And wait. And wait. Eventually you may find you need to use the facilities, and your only option is: the bathroom on the train. But before you can use the train bathroom, you need to find the car that has one. You will probably have to leave your belongings while you search for the bathroom. When you do find it, be prepared to wait in line. If you want to avoid using the train bathroom, you will have to wait until you reach the station when the train finally starts running again. If the delay is for a lengthy period of time, you won't be the only one rushing to the restroom when the train finally arrives. And in the ultimate addition of insult to injury, you may get to the station on your delayed train, rush to the restroom, and reach it just when they are closed for service or maintenance. Then what do you do? My advice, do as mom always taught you, and "go before you go."

All these tips may seem like common sense, but they are hard and fast lessons that bear repeating. When you prepare for success by following these few simple suggestions, you set yourself up for a much more comfortable, much less stressful train commuting experience. Just ask the guy who was running to catch the train...and missed.

12. The Quest Begins

Now that you have your coffee and donut, packed your entertainment of choice, and used the facilities, you are ready to begin the quest for the perfect seat, YOUR seat. Keep in mind, this is where you will spend the next minutes or hours of your life, multiplied over days, months...perhaps even years. I've known Daily Doublers who honestly feel their day is incomplete if they do not score their favorite seat on the morning train. The comfort of your gluteus maximus is of prime importance. But before you can find that seat and experience the nirvana of train travel, there is another thing to consider. You need to find the right train car.

You are probably saying to yourself, why the heck do I care what car I am in? You probably figure this is unimportant, silly, and STUPID! I mean a train car is a train car, right? *Au contraire, mon ami!* All train cars are not created equal, and much depends upon this decision. The experienced train rider knows this. Tell a Daily Doubler that it does not matter what car you are in, and they will look at you like you just crawled out from under a rock. And you will know that you have just ceded an important point of strategy to a person who will gladly take it from you. He is your competition, he is armed with the tools needed to make the right car selection, and he now sees your weakness. As a novice train rider, you are a mere babe in the woods, you know nothing! The only thing you have going for you is sheer dumb luck. So, in the words of the immortal Harry Callahan, I ask you, "Do you feel lucky? Well, do you, punk?" Of course you don't.

But take heart, all is not lost! I am relaying to you the secret to choosing the right car for you right here, in these next few paragraphs. With this valuable information, you will level the playing field. By following these tips, you can defeat your worthy opponent in the car selection round and proudly move onto the next round, seat selection.

You are ready to enter the field of battle, face down your competition. Hold your head up high, be confident. You are ready. Now let's get started.

There are several factors to consider when choosing the right car for you.

Factor # 1: Point of Exit

It may not seem important, but basing your car selection on where you wish to exit the train can be wise. For example, when you arrive in Grand Central Station, you may need to head either uptown or downtown. Grand Central has exits in both directions. When Metro North trains arrive, it could be advantageous to sit in a car towards the rear of the train, if you will be headed uptown. By doing so, you will be closer to the uptown exits from the station. If headed downtown, you should sit near the front. This will shorten your walk once you get off the train, and allow you to beat, or at least flow with, the crowds of people who are heading in the same direction.

I found that choosing the right car on my commute home was just as important. When I got off the train at my home station in Milford, I would have to walk to the nearest staircase from the platform to the parking lot. This may not seem like a big deal, and in our current sedentary lifestyle, exercise is good, right? But if it is raining or snowing, or if your walk to your car is lengthy, being in the train car that is closest to the stairwell can be a huge advantage. This was one change I made quickly. While others huddled under their umbrellas or pulled their coats over their heads, and hustled to get to the stairs in a growing crowd of people, I calmly exited the train car and descended the stairs.

Factor # 2: The Bar Car

Sounds great, huh? The Bar Car. With seats, drinks, and snacks, it may be just the place you want to be, especially at the end of a long day. But beware pinning your hopes to this oasis of convivial enjoyment. Not every train line features a bar car, and those that do have one don't always provide one on every train. Also, it is not consistently located in the same position. Sorry, no tips here--if you wish to make this your favorite spot, you will have to find it yourself. Keep in mind though, that valuable time can be lost if it turns out that your train does not have a bar car, yet you spent time looking for it. This may result in your having to take any seat you can find. Just be prepared.

Factor #3: Rest Room Car

Similar to the Bar Car, not every car has a rest room and the one that does is not always located in the same position. My advice to you is to avoid this car unless you really, REALLY think you will need it. Think about this for a moment. The scent of antiseptic chemicals that permeates the air is incentive enough for most riders to shun this car at all costs. However, if you are running late and having difficulty finding a seat, beggars can't be choosers. Look in this car. You will have a much better chance of finding an available seat there. Enough said on this one.

Factor #4: Observe Others

Creatures of habit, remember? It is likely you will see the same people in the same car every time you travel. You may find that this may not be to your liking. During my travels as a Stealth Rider, I did not have any idea what car I wanted to ride in. I did not care, just got on the darn train and grabbed a seat. When I became a Daily Doubler, I initially decided to get on a car in the middle of the train. No particular reason. I quickly found that this was a popular car for several high school students that took the train to school. That was a mistake.

Now, don't get me wrong. They're not bad kids, and they were certainly not doing anything I didn't do or at least consider in my own halcyon teenage years. We all remember our high school days, how cool we were and how cooler we were going to get. WRONG! SO wrong! Watching these young people made me realize how old I had become. And I realized that high school antics, for me, were better left to memory lane, not accompanying my commute.

I decided to move to another car. I moved to the front car where I found a larger population of grownups, and a much shorter walk when I arrived at Grand Central.

Now that you understand the importance of selecting the proper train car, I have a few tips for waiting on the platform.

Tip # 1: Know Where to Stand

Knowing where to stand is one of the most important tips I can offer you. Quite often, there are not enough seats for everyone. You will want to be first in line, or close to it, in order to get a seat, and improve the odds of getting your seat. I have found that trains typically stop at the same spot. It won't take long for you to determine exactly where the doors will open. Get to the platform early enough so that you can claim that spot.

I recall one winter morning, when I got to the platform, a lady standing in THAT spot. I had not seen her before and was not sure if she knew that she had claimed the prime territory. Moving to another spot where another door would open, maybe even a different car was an option. But I couldn't, I was a creature of habit. I had to get on THAT car. So I did the next best thing, I planted myself to her left, close enough so that no one else could get between us, but allowing enough room with respect to her personal space.

Standing just a few feet away from us were a couple reporters from a local paper. As we stood there trying to keep warm, and pointedly but cordially avoiding any conversation (we knew the rules, after all, we were both Daily Doublers), I heard one of the reporters ask my neighbor if she would answer a few questions. She graciously accepted and stepped over to speak with them in privacy. The prime spot had been vacated. I guess any respectable person would have left it that way, knowing she would be back. NOT me! I slyly took a step to my right and laid claim. If the train had arrived in the next minute, I would have been able to board quickly and my sin would be erased in the inevitable press of the crowd. But it didn't.

The interview ended, the woman returned, and I heard her voice say, "I see you took my spot." That comment alone reinforced my thinking that she was not a Day Tripper or Stealth Rider. She was a Daily Doubler and she knew the game. Making every effort not to sound like a second-grader or an inconsiderate boor, I sheepishly said, "Oh no, not at all. I was keeping it safe for you, so no one else would take it. Here you go," as I stepped back to the left. You can no doubt imagine my extreme embarrassment and feeling of foolishness. Luckily, she was not upset. She knew exactly what I was trying to pull, but accepted my weak explanation and reclaimed her spot without recrimination. She even gave me some tips that I had not known before.

We actually became commuter friends, as we had similar routines for our morning commute. You'll find this is one of the fun quirks of commuting—you'll make friends who know everything there is to know about you within the confines of your shared commute. Much like you have "work" friends", you may find that you make "commute" friends. You will become close to people you never considered for friends, and have incredibly entertaining and rewarding conversations with them. During some rides we would sit together and play the people-observing game together. Her commute was only half of mine, she worked in Stamford, CT. This left me with enough time to catch my nap into Grand Central and still be ready for my day ahead. This woman's name was Caitlyn, and perhaps someday she will read this book and recall our first meeting with a laugh. But probably not, she has probably made a new "train friend" by now and tossed her memory of me on the scrap heap.

Tip # 2: Watch The Gap

"Watch the gap" (or its British sister, "Mind the gap") is a favorite phrase of train aficionados. You may see signs and hear announcements to WATCH THE GAP! The famed gap is the space between the edge of the platform and the train car. It can be up to several inches wide, and you would do well to follow the directives and watch it! Never stand close to the edge of the platform. Makes sense, right? The obvious reason is to avoid getting caught in the gap or hit by the train. In addition, some trains may not stop at your station. And when a train passes by without slowing, the force of the wind it generates can be powerful. So please stand back from the edge.

But there is another reason for standing back from the edge, and it does not involve danger to life or limb, but it can save you no little annoyance if you remember it and conduct yourself accordingly. On one sunny summer morning, I was standing on the platform. I was now a Daily Doubler and very comfortable in my routine. I had finished my coffee, used the restroom, and packed my newspaper and music with headphones. I had claimed the prime spot on the platform. Everything was in my favor. As I stood there waiting, I noticed a smudge on my glasses.

I could not have such a smudge obscuring my vision and perhaps hurting my chances of claiming my favorite seat. I had everything else in perfect alignment for this goal! So, I removed my glasses, pulled a handkerchief from my pocket, and began to wipe my glasses clean. Suddenly, I felt something lightly glance off my hand. I looked down and saw that one of the arms had fallen off my glasses. The screw must have come loose and my cleaning of the glasses caused the screw and arm to fall off.

I looked at my feet to find the arm, and hopefully the screw, but no luck. I could not find either. Then, I looked over the edge and saw down there, lying on the track was the arm to my glasses. I had not watched the gap! And now, a piece that was essential to my glasses (which are essential to my vision and my ability to function as an independent person) was there, lost forever in that perilous gap.

Staring at it, I considered for a moment: I *could jump down onto the tracks, retrieve the arm, and climb back up.* But the drop was about 5 feet. I probably would break my ankle landing in the uneven gravel that lay between the rails. And, how would I get back up on the platform? There were no stairs and I doubt anyone would risk pulling me up for fear of falling onto the tracks themselves. And what if a train came along while I was on the tracks? Is that the way I want to die, squashed like a bug as I chased after a piece of plastic? And if I did in fact survive and retrieve the precious piece, what laws would I be breaking? The signs posted clearly state that entry onto the tracks is forbidden. Seemed like a big risk to take just to salvage the arm of my glasses. I decided to leave it be.

The question now was, what do I do? As Fearless Fly (a popular kids cartoon back in the day) would say, "without my glasses I am helpless." I would have to go home and take the day off to get a replacement. But that would likely take a few days as it would have to be ordered. And how would I even drive? I imagined having to pull Corinne out of work like a 7-year-old with a stomach bug, explaining the situation and pleading, "Please come and pick me up!" That would not go over well. She'd probably ask why I wasn't watching the gap! While I stood there, feeling foolish and pondering my next move, my new train friend Caitlyn arrived on the platform. I told her what happened and relayed my dilemma. After her initial reaction (gales of laughter) subsided, she suggested an idea I had not thought of, blinded by panic as I was. After exiting the train, I could walk to a drug store and buy a pair of "cheater" glasses (you know, the kind that people buy to help them read.) GENIUS! I was saved. But it taught me an important lesson.

STAY AWAY FROM THE EDGE OF THE PLATFORM!
WATCH THE GAP!

13. Ok, I'm On The Train, Now What?

It's a cold, cold winter morning. You wake up in the comfort of your own bed, snuggle up to keep warm, and dream of hitting the snooze button just one more time. But alas, you must get up and begin your day.

Fast forward an hour or so, and you are wrapped in layers of clothing, hoping to stay warm while you listen for the piercing sound of the train horn as it approaches the station. You took heed of the tips in chapters 11 and 12, packing lightly and laying claim to the best spot on the platform. When the train arrives and the door opens, you will be the first to enter the warmth and comfort that you eagerly await. It is the only thing on your mind right now. You think to yourself, if I can just get on the train, I don't care about anything else.

But, there is more to your trip. It really has not yet even begun. So while the others around you are shivering with the cold weather and the anxiety of the impending train boarding, it is time for you to start planning your next move. What do you do when you board the train? It is not just about getting warmed up. It's about finding your seat.

After hearing of my day in the city with my in-laws, several of my nephews decided that they would like to go visit Ground Zero. They were young at the time of 9/11 and had grown up in the world we all faced in its aftermath. So, once again, I took another precious vacation day and used it, not to sleep in and get some work done around my house or yard, but to make my same two and a half hour commute to lower Manhattan. But this time with my sister Martha, her son and a friend of his, and my brother Andy's three boys.

We arrived at the train station on a cold, wet, rainy morning, hoping that the weatherman's promise of clearing skies would come true. Walking the caverns of New York City is not my favorite thing to do when the winds are cold and blowing. We parked the car and scaled the stairs to the platform. Although I was armed with my trusty monthly pass, my six companions (5 of whom had never ridden the train before) needed to purchase tickets. Being the veteran of the group, I took charge at the kiosk. It was now <u>my</u> turn to fumble my way through the ticket purchasing process, knowing that other riders were anxiously waiting their turn. After several restarts, I was able to complete the task at hand.

We migrated from the kiosk to my favorite waiting place on the platform; the place where I waited every day, where the doors would open wide and we would be the first to enter the train. I was anxious to get my charges on board and seated together. This was a commuter train that would be filled with Daily Doublers, and I knew it was likely we would be scattered among different seats. Leading the charge. I entered the train car followed by my five soldiers with my sister bringing up the rear.

Fortunately, I spotted a 2-seater on the left side of the train car, and two 3-seaters across the aisle. Perfect! Martha and I could sit together and the boys could mix and match however they chose. What a relief, just grab a seat and park it! But as I entered my row and turned to direct the others, I heard one of the boys mutter something I had never heard on the train before. I looked back to the aisle and there was my nephew, staring at his ticket and asking himself, "now what seat is mine?". See, he assumed there was assigned seating and he was looking on his ticket for a row and seat number. In retrospect, this was understandable. He had never ridden a train before but had flown in an airplane many times. It made sense to him that he would be assigned a seat.

Now, in the grand scheme of things this may not seem like a big deal. But remember, although I was a Day Tripper on this day, I am a Daily Doubler at heart. I could not deny my sensitivities. As my nephew stared at his ticket, I looked behind him, only to see the line of Daily Doublers standing still, waiting for him to make his move so that they may then find their own seat and settle in. I responded quickly and told my nephew, SIT ANYHWERE!

So now that you know you can choose your seat, there are several factors and decisions that go into choosing the right seat for you. After reading about these factors, you will know what is best for you. Then you can apply the tips that follow to help you find that seat.

Factor #1: Face Forward Or Backward

Some train cars offer seats facing in both directions. If you are not affected by the direction you face, then this may not matter to you. But some people feel nausea when they ride facing backwards. Those people must consider this factor carefully in order to avoid getting sick and being the center of a very embarrassing episode.

Factor #2: Facing The Sun

Depending on the time of day and the location of the sun in the sky, you could end up sitting with the sun shining brightly in your eyes. If you intend to sleep, or just prefer to avoid the potential discomfort of a blinding eyeful of direct sunlight, consider sitting where this is least possible to happen. And always bring your sunglasses.

Factor #3: Restroom Facilities

In the previous chapter, I discussed avoiding this car if you can. However, if you have just left the company holiday party, or spent an exciting evening in the city eating and carousing, you may find that you need to use these facilities sometime during your ride. So the restroom car would be an ideal choice for you. However, having made this assessment for yourself, your next decision will be to figure out exactly where in this car you wish to sit.

Factor #4: Leg Room

Think about how much legroom you require. The car may have a limited number of seats with extra legroom. If you don't absolutely need a seat with extra legroom, try to leave it available for someone who does. Think of taller people, who would have to endure the train ride with their legs folded up like a jackknife if forced to sit in a regular seat, or a handicapped person that may benefit from the extra room.

Factor #5: Traveling With Others

If you are traveling with others, you may wish to consider sitting in a space where the seats face each other. This will allow you to carry on conversations face-to-face and hopefully, with less intrusion to other passengers. But be aware, you may have less legroom and you will be competing with the person sitting across from you for that valuable commodity.

Now that you have defined your own personal preferences according to these factors, here are some tips to follow when choosing your own personal seat. One point to keep in mind, your train most likely has open seating. In other words, you are not assigned a seat. You can choose whatever seat is available. Obviously, if your train does have assigned seating, then these tips won't matter. I have never been on a train with assigned seating, because typically commuter trains are open seating (read: every man or woman for themselves!) A first-class train ticket generally buys you a reserved seat, but this is a coach commuter train I'm talking about, it's a democratic society with survivalist elements. No caste system here. Long distance trains do offer cars with assigned seating, for obvious reasons—I mean, you don't want to be sleeping in your sleeper car and have some complete stranger roust you out of bed and challenge you to a fight for the next leg of the trip from New York to Chicago!

Tip #1: Which Side Of The Train

The side of the train that you sit on can be very important if the sun is a concern for you. The Metro-North train line that I commuted on traveled along the southern Connecticut coast in an east to west direction (ok, more like northeast to southwest). After some experimentation, I found that the sun tended to shine in the windows on the south side of the train cars in the morning and the north side during the commute home. Since sleeping was my main concern, I preferred to avoid the direct sunlight. Thus I sat on the opposite side from where the sunlight shone. Of course, if you travel during the hours of darkness, this will not apply to you and you can blissfully ignore it. And on days of rain, snow, or just clouds, this is not an issue either. Hey! I knew I could think of a positive thing about bad weather!

Tip # 2: 2 Seats Or 3

You may find that your train has two seats on one side of the train and three on the other. When I first started traveling, I did not have a preference one way or the other if I sat in a row that had two or three seats. It was my train partner Caitlyn who told me, if given a choice, to always take the 3-seater. Her reasoning was, there is a better chance that you won't have someone sit right next to you, as long as you sit in the aisle seat or next to the window. People don't like to squeeze into the middle seat if they don't have to. Of course, if the train is crowded, they may have no choice. But if the middle seat does not become occupied, you can use it to store your extra baggage (remember be kind and share with your neighbor on the other side of the empty seat). Also, you will have more legroom.

Tip #3: Aisle Or Window Seat

Regardless whether you choose a 2-seater or 3-seater row, you now need to decide if you prefer to sit on the aisle or by the window. Yes, in a 3-seater you can choose the middle seat. But I can't think why anyone would do so unless it was the only one open. However, if all 3 seats are open, by selecting the center seat, you may discourage anyone from sitting next to you and you could end up with the whole row (and a less-than-stellar reputation).

The choice of aisle or window is up to you. Some people prefer the aisle so that they can quickly exit the train. They are not forced to wait for others in the row to exit. Others prefer the window. It allows for more seclusion. Sitting by the window, you are not disturbed by the traffic moving through the aisle each time the train makes a stop, or the conductors passing through the car to take tickets. Because sleeping was one of my favorite pastimes for the train ride, you can easily guess where I sat. Another advantage to the window on the Metro-North cars was the existence of a small shelf that ran along the sidewall of the train. I suppose it encloses something important to the running or the inner workings of the train. But for me, it was a place to put my foot and enhance my own personal comfort. So take a look for that nice little advantage.

Tip #4: Look Under The Seat In Front Of Yours

I found this tip to be one of the most overlooked (at least by me) and yet it can be one of the most important. As you walk down the aisle searching for your preferred seat, be sure to look under the seat in front of the one you have chosen. It is possible that you will find that someone else has left his or her trash there. I have seen newspapers, food wrappers, empty cups and bottles. Even worse, I have seen cups that still contain their drink. The last thing you want is to have that spill on your feet. It should be pointed out that the people that work on the trains strive to keep them clean, and they are doing an excellent job by anyone's standards. However, we've already established that trains are can consist of many cars, and it is not possible to go through every car and clean up after every single stop to catch the debris from that one irresponsible rider.

Another reason to look under the seat in front of you has nothing to do with trash left behind. On some of the trains that I commuted on, there are some seats that have a metal box beneath them that were attached to the floor. I suspect these boxes had to do with the heating and cooling system, which of course makes them eminently important. No matter, the thing about this box that annoyed me was that it was immovable (I assume, I did not try to move it for fear of disturbing some incredibly sensitive equipment and upsetting the balance of the train's indoor temperature) and reduced the legroom considerably. So be sure to look first before taking a seat, to check if the box or other obstruction is under the seat in front of yours.

Tip #5: Watch Out For The Other Guy

All the best planning in the world can be quashed by the random actions of another person. Remember my discussion in chapter 7 about the Day Tripper. This person will likely board the train and take any seat available. They are unaware of the factors you have studied, and therefore the quest for the perfect seat will be wasted on them. You can avoid the frustration of losing your version of seating nirvana to a rider who has no idea of its true value, by entering the train first, as we discussed in chapter 12.

Finally, you have found your seat and nestled into it, ready for your journey. You are confined to this relatively small area, packed in like a can of sardines. It is important to create an environment where everyone gets along and travels without incident. It is time for train etiquette suggestions to kick into gear.

Basic rule of thumb: Be considerate of other travelers.

14. You've made It! You Have Arrived!

It's a beautiful day here in the Caribbean. The sand is as soft as baby powder, the sky is blue and the water crystal clear. I smile, recalling childhood beach vacations, as I hear the sound of the waves as they strike the beach along with the chatter of young children playing in the sand.

Wait! What was that?

Who said that?

What did I just hear?

"Attention, the next stop is Grand Central, it is the last stop, please be sure to take all your belongings."

Where am I? Where did the beach go? Wait a minute... I was... dreaming?

The salty sea air is quickly replaced by the smell of machinery as we pull into the bowels of the station. My ears are now assaulted by loud public announcements, rather than being tickled with the soft crash of waves and the babble of little children at play. Yawning, I try to collect my belongings and my wits simultaneously, and make my way out of the cozy confines of the train car and onto the platform. The peaceful tranquility of my Caribbean beach vision grows faint, as I join the hustle and bustle of commuters rushing to their next destination.

Such is the risk of sleeping on the train. Your dreams can offer a pleasant break from the reality of the day ahead, but waking up and realizing that it was all a dream can be quite unsettling. Your train ride has ended. Now what do you do?

The good news is that you have finished the train portion of your commute. Hopefully you were able to use some of my tips and suggestions to help make your ride more comfortable. At this point you can just exit the train and move on with your day. But I do have some additional tips for the end of your train ride, and I suggest you take a look. It will allow for an easier transition from the train to re-entry into your daily life beyond your commute.

Tip #1: Expect A Rush, Be Patient

Believe it or not, you are probably <u>not</u> the only one getting off the train. Daily Doublers are trying to get to work on time. If you do not have a time constraint, remain in your seat and let those that do, exit first. If you should be so lucky, use those precious seconds to meditate on the joys of life or whatever you want...just don't get in the way of a Daily Doubler on a mission, they are on a schedule and they may run you down. But, should you be seated in the aisle seat, you may need to exit in order to avoid preventing anyone next to you from exiting. They will appreciate it, and once they have hurried away, you will have the freedom to stroll at your own pace.

Tip #2: Keep Moving

Once you begin your exit, keep moving, not only along the platform but into the common area or lobby too. Quite often I have seen Day Trippers and Stealth Riders stop suddenly, probably to get their bearings and figure out which direction to go, or just to look at their watch. When they do this, the crowd of people walking behind them must also stop, and suddenly we are treated to a spectacle not unlike the moment at the circus when the clowns start coming out and falling over one another. It's funny at the circus, but aggravating at the train station. If you are lost and really need to stop and gather your thoughts, step to the side, out of the way of the people behind you. If possible, zero in on a secluded area and go there. If you stop right where you are, you may get trampled and cause a great deal of irritation and injury to others.

Collisions on the platform can turn dangerous and are not uncommon. After a long, uneventful ride, the last thing you want is to get into a dispute because of something that you could have easily avoided by taking two steps aside from the crowd.

Tip #3: Take Your Turn

If, on the other hand, you are in a hurry and must exit as quickly as possible, you too should remember to be courteous. Rows should empty in sequence, beginning with the rows closest to the exit. If allowed, you may wait in the vestibule (area near the train door) so that you can exit quickly.

Tip #4: Stay Awake

This should go without saying, right? Well, I used to think so, too. If your destination is the last stop on the trip, then it's just fine. Everyone has to get off. The train stops. If you are sleeping, it is likely the rush of others will wake you, or if you are sleeping deeply, the train conductor certainly will. But, if your stop is not the last one and you like to sleep to pass the time, you could risk sleeping through your stop. As your mother probably said to you growing up, *"I won't be always around to wake you up for school in the morning!"*

I can speak for the last tip with my own personal experience. As you know by now, sleeping is what I like to do to get through the trip. I knew the risks, and I followed the rules. But on two occasions, I slept through my stop on my return trip at the end of the day. I usually read for 20 minutes, then turned on my music, put on my sunglasses, and fell asleep. My morning commutes ended in Grand Central and on many occasions I slept all the way there. No problem! It was the last stop, the train halted, and I woke up and exited, albeit a little drowsily.

Such was not always the case for my return trip. On one occasion after a long day at work and joining several of my office compadres for a post-work social gathering at a nearby watering hole, I arrived at Grand Central for my long ride home. As it was later in the evening, I took an off-peak train and was surprised at how full this train was. The combination of an exhausting day and a jovial "happy hour" proved my undoing. I had no interest in following my normal routine, which called for me to read for a while. I waited until the conductor took my ticket, then closed my eyes, grateful to be headed home. I was out in a flash.

This was possibly the deepest sleep I ever experienced on the train. I am not sure what caused me to wake, but when I did, it was sudden. I could feel the train come to a stop, and then quickly begin to move again. I immediately sat up straight and looked out my window, hoping to recognize the town we were leaving and praying it was one that preceded my stop. Peering out the window into the dark, still in a bit of a daze from my deep sleep, I struggled to recognize the surrounding grounds of the station as we pulled away. After a few moments, I glimpsed the center of town and knew immediately it was my own! I had missed my stop.

After I got over my aggravation, realizing I had no one to blame but myself, I began to consider my options. I could ask the conductor to back up and let me off. At that moment I was sure he would have been happy to do so. What's the big deal, stopping a train and backing it up a couple miles? And I was sure my fellow passengers would not mind. Adding another fifteen minutes or so to their commute would be fine with them, right? Okay, maybe not. It became quickly clear to me that I had no options, other than to get off at the next stop and catch the next train back.

The good news was that I could use my monthly ticket, saving the cost of an additional ticket. The bad news was that the next train did not leave for about an hour. And by now, I desperately wanted to get home. So I decided to take a taxi. So much for saving money. This was probably the first time I truly appreciated the existence of ATM machines. See, I did not have enough cash to pay the cabbie. And the poor guy had no change, of course—why should he, when his main source of income came from fools like me? I must have been his first fare of the evening. Right! I had to have the cab driver take me to an ATM so I could get money to pay him. And since ATMs only pay out in $20 bills, you can guess how big a tip he got. After that experience, I always made sure I had enough cash with me on future rides. If this ever happened again, I would be prepared. AND IT DID (and I was)!

15. Tourists Are People Too

There you have it! I hope these tips and suggestions help to make your train ride more comfortable and enjoyable. While these are based on my experience as a Daily Doubler, Day Trippers and Stealth Riders can use many of them too.

As a Daily Doubler, it was very clear to me that commuters made up the majority of riders during normal workdays. Sure, there were tourists scattered throughout the crowd but the commuters dominated the train population. Behaving like a typical Daily Doubler was easy, it was the norm. But don't think for one moment that I am insensitive to other train riders. In fact, after reading through these pages and reliving my commuting experience, I remembered my own excitement at taking the train for pleasure trips. I have taken the train into New York as a Day Tripper on several occasions, starting before I even knew what a Day Tripper was. But after becoming a regular commuter and developing my own personal traveling strategy, I was able to take what I'd learned as a Daily Doubler and apply it to fun trips too.

And perhaps more importantly, I was able to let go of my Daily Doubler tendencies and just enjoy the ride like a Day Tripper would. Life is not just about getting from Point A to Point B. It is truly a journey of change and we are the only ones who can choose how we view it: a journey to excitement or a trudge to work. That is why this chapter is dedicated to these travelers, the Day Trippers.

One thing I've always noted is that a train car primarily populated by Day Trippers takes on a totally different personality than that of a commuter-filled car. Daily Doublers tend to be quiet, keeping to themselves. Day Trippers bring a higher level of energy that converts the train into a more lively and noisy ride.

This was most obvious to me the day my son Ryan and I rode the train from Milford to attend a Yankees baseball game. When we boarded the train, the car was mostly empty and finding a seat was not a problem. At each stop along the way, more and more Yankee fans heading for the game boarded the train. Sporting the team colors, they were easy to spot. Many even wore the traditional pinstriped jerseys with their favorite player's name spelled out across the shoulders.

It was a treat to witness such a crowd, a living, breathing diversity of excitement and anticipation. There were old-timers, young couples, and groups of young men who probably go to every game, some who appeared to have already begun celebrating a victory, even before the game had begun. I was especially touched to see the fathers, with young children dressed like ball players and clutching their baseball glove in hopes of catching an errant ball as it sailed over the foul line or cracked off a bat for a home run. Even on the train they would not take the glove off for fear that they may misplace it and lose out on their chance for such a valued prize. Their excitement of going to their first big-league game was only heightened by the additional treat of a train ride full of fellow Yankee fans. The older fans willingly welcomed the young into the fold, remembering their own childhood experiences, sensing an obligation to help in the evolution of this new batch of recruits as true Yankee fans, all under the watchful and protective eye of the proud parents.

These people didn't care where they sat, and they didn't care about the noise. There was a common bond that brought everyone together. The level of enthusiasm only increased as the crowd did, at every stop. This adventure was early in my train riding life, before I had become a full-fledged Daily Doubler, so assimilating into this crowd was easy.

This was not the case when Corinne and I rode with our friends Janet, Ed, Eileen and Dave. Over the years the 6 of us have shared a lot of fun times. We have vacationed on Martha's Vineyard and Aruba, and cruised to Nova Scotia. We have traveled by car, chauffer-driven limo, bus, ferry boat, plane and cruise ship. On one day trip Corinne and I took our friends on our power boat, for a ride to Port Jefferson on Long Island. Now while this may not sound as thrilling as a cruise, or a week in Aruba, it did have its own brand of excitement–we had to be rescued by the Coast Guard on our return to Connecticut. But that's a story for another book, maybe.

On this cold day in December, we traveled by train to New York City. It was a Saturday during the Christmas season and the city was adorned with beautiful, colorful lights. Eileen had planned this excursion to the Big Apple. It began with all of us meeting at the home of Jan and Ed where Eileen reviewed the day's itinerary. Our expedition included a visit to the Metropolitan Museum of Art, cocktails and appetizers at Mickey Mantle's Restaurant and Sports Bar. The day wound up with dinner at Bottega DelVino. After taking lunch orders, Dave and I drove to the deli to pick up lunch for everyone; Eddie was responsible for getting the ladies to the train station where we would all meet up. Through his connections, Dave was able to secure train tickets in advance for himself and the others. I, of course, was armed with my monthly pass, which I proudly displayed. My companions were <u>not</u> impressed. Like true Day Trippers, we chatted the whole ride, ate our lunches, and solved the problems of the world.

The train was full of Day Trippers, although unlike the train ride to Yankee Stadium, each group was traveling to the city for different reasons. But while there was not a common destination, there was still the energy that can be expected when a group of festive people celebrating the holidays is drawn together. As for me, I was now a full-fledge Daily Doubler. The allure of loosening up and enjoying the total experience as a Day Tripper was tempting.

However, I was restrained by my role as a Daily Doubler. I was a "creature of habit" and could not let go of what my experiences had taught me. When we mounted the platform, I instructed my friends where to stand so that we could be first on the train when the doors opened. They looked at me as if I had suggested a wife swap, but they complied.

My strategy paid off: the train was crowded but we were able to locate seating for all six of us together. Of course, applying my "seat-finding" technique, I had my window seat on the north side of the train, avoiding direct sunlight. And during our ride home late that evening, when all of us were exhausted, I simply put on my sunglasses, turned on my music, rested my foot on the ledge under the window, slumped into my preferred sleeping position and slept all the way home while the rest of my clan fidgeted to find their comfort zone, alternating between chatting about the events of the day and catching a quick catnap. The last thing I recall was Jan questioning me as to why I was putting on my sunglasses indoors at a time when the skies were blanketed in darkness. Ah, those Day Trippers, you gotta love 'em.

Upon our return home I was lectured by my wife for my lack of manners and social skills, choosing to sleep on the ride home rather than relive the day's events with her and our friends. Refreshed by my nap, I remained unruffled by her scorn and that of our friends, who still tease me about it. Today, I am better at diplomatically sharing my Daily Doubler knowledge, because, after all, Day Trippers have their needs, too.

16. Terminus

When I began writing this book, I was not sure where it would lead me. I saw my experiences as humorous, at least to me. I was not sure others would think so. It was only after sharing some of the stories with family and friends and the encouragement from them to put these in writing, that I decided to try it. So much of the gratitude, or blame, must be shuttled their way.

At first I kept thinking of tips, ways I could offer useful information to fellow train commuters. As I began to write, more and more stories came to me. I realized this was not going to be just a book of train tips, it was becoming a book that encompassed a slice of life, my life.

I started this book by saying that life is a journey. As I wrote, I relived many experiences in my life from childhood to today. It became a journey, just as my daily commute was, and made me appreciate the journey all the more.

The first vehicle many of us rode by ourselves (baby strollers don't count, as they were navigated by our moms and dads) was our bicycle. My first 2-wheeler was green with 20" wheels. I am sure I had a tricycle (probably a hand me down from my older brother and sister) but that is where my memory ends. As I got older, my bikes got bigger. My friends and I spent many hours pedaling mile after mile. We grew up from bikes to cars, then trains, planes, and boats. And now my life has come full circle. Today, I no longer ride the train to work. And Corinne and I purchased bicycles recently. We intended to ride them as a form of exercise, but really, it's just fun to do and brings us both back to younger, carefree times. Although we are not as daring as we were as children, we now wear helmets and would never consider riding with no hands.

As we pass from one slice of life to another, there are constants that stay with us through time. We are creatures of habit. Whether it's a new morning routine that has been adjusted to changes in our daily life, or addressing the golf ball in our own unique way (hopefully NOT by saying "hello ball"), we will continue to be creatures of habit. And people-watching will continue to be a major means for passing the time.

Today's world is very different than the one I grew up in the 60's and 70's. As kids, we played outdoors every chance we could. Whether it was baseball games or sled riding down a snowy hill, we were together and we were outside. When I drive through a neighborhood nowadays, I seldom see any children outside. Neighborhood activities have been replaced by play-groups, baseball games have been replaced by video games, heck, talking on the phone has moved to text messaging. (I still can't figure that one out.) Today's children will have different kinds of memories than we had, just as our memories differed from those of our parents.

What is not going to change, though, will be transportation. Yes, there will be hybrid cars and the like, but they will still be cars. And trains, planes, boats and buses will be with us for a long, long time...I don't think we're going to be jetting around in personal space ships for a while yet, especially with the price of gas what it is. So if you have the occasion to travel by train, take a closer look at the experience. Observe your surroundings and admire the work, effort, and technology that have taken us from coal-fired steam engines to today's high-speed trains. And as you go through your life, look around, observe, adapt, and relive. Because you can't remember when you got on this train of life, and you have no control over when or how you get off. So Daily Doublers, Day Trippers and Stealth Riders alike all need to sit on the same train and enjoy the ride.

I do believe that this is possible, because I experienced it firsthand. My wife and I once rode the train to New York with friends to attend the New York Marathon. Having grown up in New York, George and Maria were accustomed to trains, and experts on finding their way around the city. But even they were not aware of the finer points of train travel. We chose to sit in 2 rows facing each other so that we could visit. Previously I told you how this seating does not allow for much legroom. As a Daily Doubler, this can be an issue. But as a Day Tripper, it is easier to let it go, especially when traveling with friends.

By the time we took this trip, Corinne had heard enough from me about the commuting experience and it was clear she was coming over to the Dark Side. (Husbands, take heart—someday you will be able to tell your wife something and have her actually agree with you and take your advice. I am living proof.) Unbeknownst to me, she had even prepared for the trip by following some of my tips. For one, she brought her own music. On our way to the station, she started talking to me about where the sun would be in the sky, and once we boarded, she chose our seats accordingly. In fact, all four seats were shielded from direct sunlight.

As a Daily Doubler, I'd never been so proud. Tears of joy came to my eyes as I realized I'd converted her to the basic tenets of commuter train travel. When we boarded the train for the long ride home, after an eventful day in the city, I watched as my Day Tripper wife settled into her well-chosen seat, put on her headphones, and bade me, "sweet dreams, honey."

I knew it would be a pleasant ride.